SENSITIVE SKIN

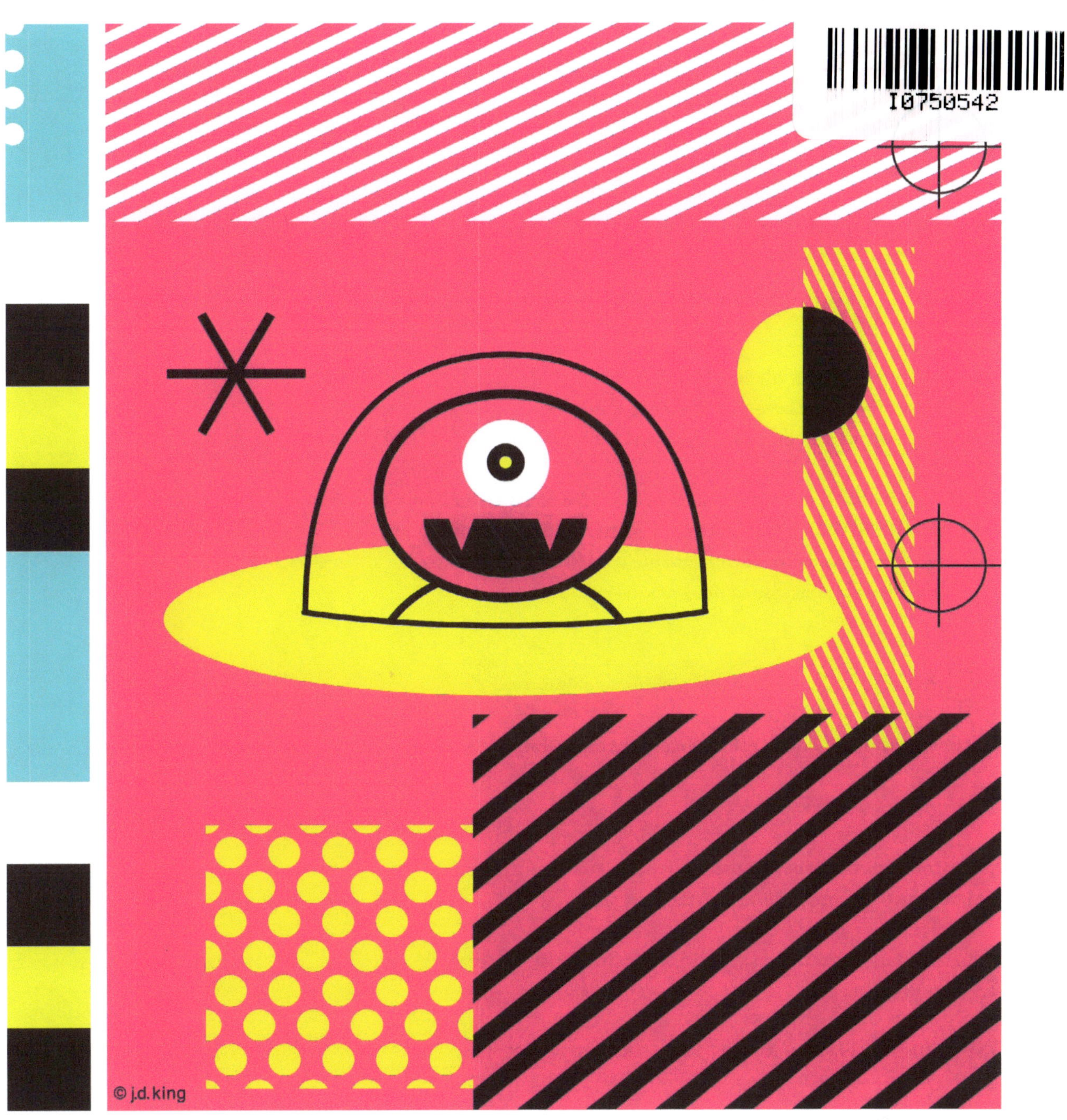

Sensitive Skin Magazine is also available online at **www.sensitiveskinmagazine.com.**

Publisher/Managing Editor: Bernard Meisler
Associate Editors: Rob Hardin, Mike DeCapite & B. Kold
Music Editor: Steve Horowitz
Contributing Editors: Ron Kolm & Tim Beckett

This issue is dedicated to Chris Bava.

Front cover: *Prime Directive,* by J.D. King
Back cover: James Romberger

You can find us at:
Facebook—**www.facebook.com/sensitiveskin**
Twitter—**www.twitter.com/sensitivemag**
YouTube—**www.youtube.com/sensitiveskintv**

We also publish in various electronic formats (Kindle, iOS, etc.), and have our own line of books. For more info about **Sensitive Skin** in other formats, **Sensitive Skin Books**, and books, films and music by our contributors, please go to **www.sensitiveskinmagazine.com/store**. To purchase back issues in print format, go to **www.sensitiveskinmagazine.com/back-issues**.

You can contact us at **info@sensitiveskinmagazine.com**.

Submissions: **www.sensitiveskinmagazine.com/submissions**.

ISBN-10: 0-9839271-6-2
ISBN-13: 978-0-9839271-6-7

Contents

The Forgetting of Water

Doug Rice

Mai struggles to experience the place of words in her body. The slow patience of her tongue, of her lips. The care she gives to each letter, the way each letter shapes her mouth. Each word changes her. This foreign tongue she now speaks as if it were her mother tongue.

J'ai toujours aime l'eau passionnement.

Mai tortures words. Teases them with tender slips of her tongue. She only speaks around the edges of letters. Innocent, yet punished like trees after a torrential rain and windstorm. Ripped from their place of stillness.

Beneath her language another language haunts her. One more agile, one more ancient, one more elusive. She tells me that words from these places can barely be spoken. This is the language of our lungs, a breath that pries open our lips. *Qu' est-ce qu'une priere?* Climbing mountains in Vietnam, Mai walked on the bones of her ancestors. With each footstep over the dry earth, the rocks, she felt her ancestors cry. Her ancestors repeatedly told Mai to be careful around those who claim to know the history of fire and yet remain unafraid of rain.

Mai and I crossed into each other's languages. Obeying only those words that haunted us.

Tongue.

Finger.

Lips.

The brail of this loving. She only wished to dominate desire.

Mai contemplates her wounds. Only damaged skin can seduce her body. Torn flesh. She cuts straight lines across her wrists. She cuts as deep as she can so each cut will become a scar. Most memories remain silent. Siren songs to herself.

The tip of each finger as precise, as agile, as an eyelid.

Maia's body waits for the sun to vanish behind the clouds. Her fingers childish and curious pulling blackberries from a bush. "All through the foothills of Vietnam," she tells Doug, "there are people whose skin is made of rain. Some say such people are only the people of myth, of old stories dropped along the way, the wet underside of river rocks." Her eyes witness the appearance of these words, her words, her breath, her dreaming. "These people say this as if myths were not true, as if the people of myths were not real. But I have met these people. I have touched the water of their skin. I have listened to their damp voices, their whispers, their murmuring sentences."

Once upon a time, we are told a story of a day before the war ended. She says, "You see only her trace." He says, "You have not forgotten enough."

This woman remembered the fear more than the pain. And she remembered the blackberry bushes cutting into her ankles more than the pain that she knows she will never speak of.

She screamed at this pain, screamed against this pain, screamed into this pain to make it go away but it never went away. Ever. Even now. Even in this moment.

Imagine a butterfly being pinned to a board. That tiny cry of terror suffocated beneath glass.

Some man blindfolded this woman, then pushed her down into the mud. She did all she could to remember that day long ago, before those bombs began falling down on her village, before she and her people dug tunnels, before they learned this new way for breathing, before she broke her fingernails clawing at the dry dirt. She did all she could to remember that day she picked herself up out of the earth.

She imagined she was made of water.

Then someone with soft hands, a young girl perhaps, undressed this woman. The woman listened to the child's soft crying as this child unbuttoned what remained of this woman's blouse. The woman wanted to comfort the child, to whisper a prayer, a chant, but this woman can no longer speak. Her tongue has been burned by coals.

This woman moved her fingers to lightly touch this child's hair to let the child know there is always hope, that trees reach up from the earth to touch the sky.

Naked.

The child's touch abandoned this woman.

Callused hands grabbed the woman's wrists, pulled them behind her back. Bound them with rope.

Nineteen years of innocence but now this woman's fingers break. Now her wrists burn. Now her strong tongue touches the roof of her dry silent mouth.

Maybe so she will not forget, she falls asleep.

Mai contemplates her wounds. Only damaged skin can seduce her body. Torn flesh. She cuts straight lines across her wrists. She cuts as deep as she can so each cut will become a scar. Most memories remain

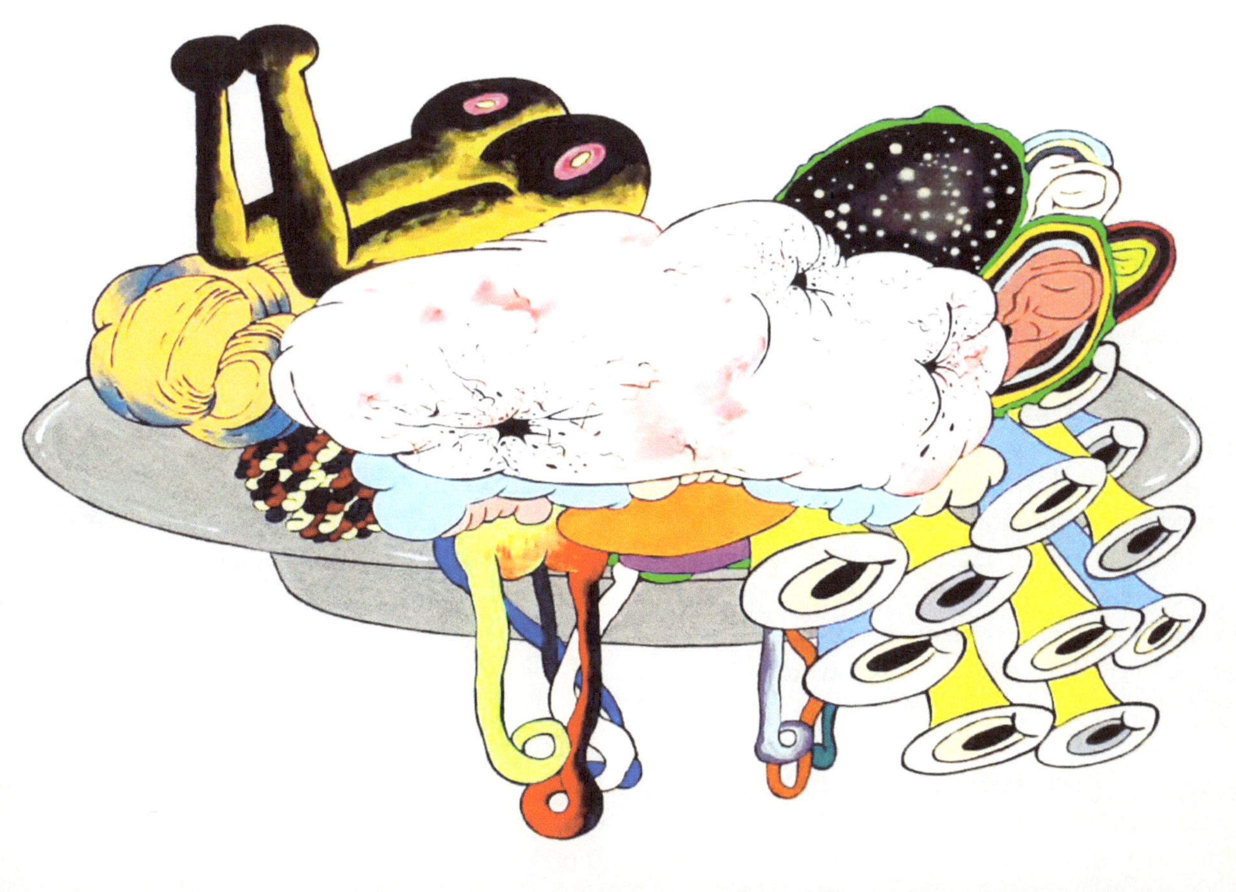

What You Eat II, acrylic on polyester, HaYoung Kim, 2012

silent. Siren songs to herself.

When she speaks of home, Maia tastes those fires on her tongue, and her words turn to ash.

She wept. On her knees. At the river.

The blood of Mai's ancestors ran through her syllables. Her mother, when Mai was still an infant, warned Mai that if she ever bit into her tongue, she could poison herself with her past, the stories from before she was born. But Mai thought biting her tongue would release the stories of her ancestors into her body, into her desire. So she bit and bit until the blood from her bleeding appeared.

Her tongue, heavy, swollen with centuries of words, of wounds, of sacrificial petals from the Lotus flower, bled into her voice.

Her tongue, heavy, swollen with centuries of words, of wounds, of sacrificial petals from the Lotus flower, bled into her voice.

Mai speaks confusing tender words, prattles in tongues that war against each other—the home tongue of her grandmother bombed to pieces by this tongue she has adopted in exile.

Mutilated words made out of the bones of her ancestors fall from Mai's lips.

Speaking in the tongue of her mother, Mai's soft voice becomes the song of a sparrow lost among tree branches. Other women from those same hills in Binh Dinh spoke in the tender spirit of butterfly wings. Veiled whispers beneath quilts. The need to survive in quiet movements. The longing to continue their stories. Each story one of flight through the trees to the plains, to the rivers, to the oceans. In the loud streets of San Francisco, people ridicule her gentle voice, a voice that releases words with such care that the air remains still around her mouth. They say her savage mouth will never understand their language. Her teachers demand that she speak like a human. Children in her class place boats made out of newspapers on her tiny school desk. It is darker than any darkness when her family pushes their unsteady boat into the water. Inside this darkness, they fear lighting their bamboo lanterns, and when their eyes close to sleep, to dream, to collapse, they are haunted by a fear that they will live inside this darkness for the rest of their lives. This water, all this water, this ocean must end, but her family, so quiet, can no longer find their faith, only splinters in their fingers and persistent small pains in their strong feet. They want to disappear beyond the dark, fall off some unknown horizon. And they fear arriving as much as they fear drowning. They speak to each other through the songs of those nearly forgotten sparrows so their voices are not heard. Ever. They dream the only dream they can remember, a dream of becoming birds, spirit birds nearly invisible in the night sky, more dangerous than dreams. In some other world, where such birds cannot be heard, where birds are not listened to, an uncle, holding paper names tight in a small fist, waits on dry land.

Mai dreamt with her tongue.

Pomegranate seeds between her teeth.
Persimmon flesh between her fingers.
Between.
Her knees held tight.
Her thighs bruised and tired.
A stray thumb near her lips
Presses.
There is nothing in between.
A thumbprint.

In fire, words become cinders. They wait in the foothills in southern Vietnam for fertilizing rains. Mai waits with them. Waits. She longed to cry, but she lived in a body without water, without breath. She slept, slowly, as if she had never been born.

Shadows never leave scars no matter where they touch you. It is as if the shadow never touched your skin to begin with, as if the shadow were only an apparition.

(an excerpt from *Between Appear and Disappear)*

Sucker

Susan Scutti

I WAS WALKING ALONG THE SOUTH SIDE OF Houston, heading home from a friend's house. I'd stopped by to pick up my copy of *The Big Sleep*, one of many loaned-and-borrowed books between us. I was living on Prince Street then, a studio on the top floor at the back of a building between Mott and Elizabeth. (From one of my two windows I could see into the sculpture garden on Elizabeth.) It was beginning to get dark and the weather was extremely cold. I was just outside that knish place tucked in the strip of stores between Katz's Deli and the Bowery when I saw

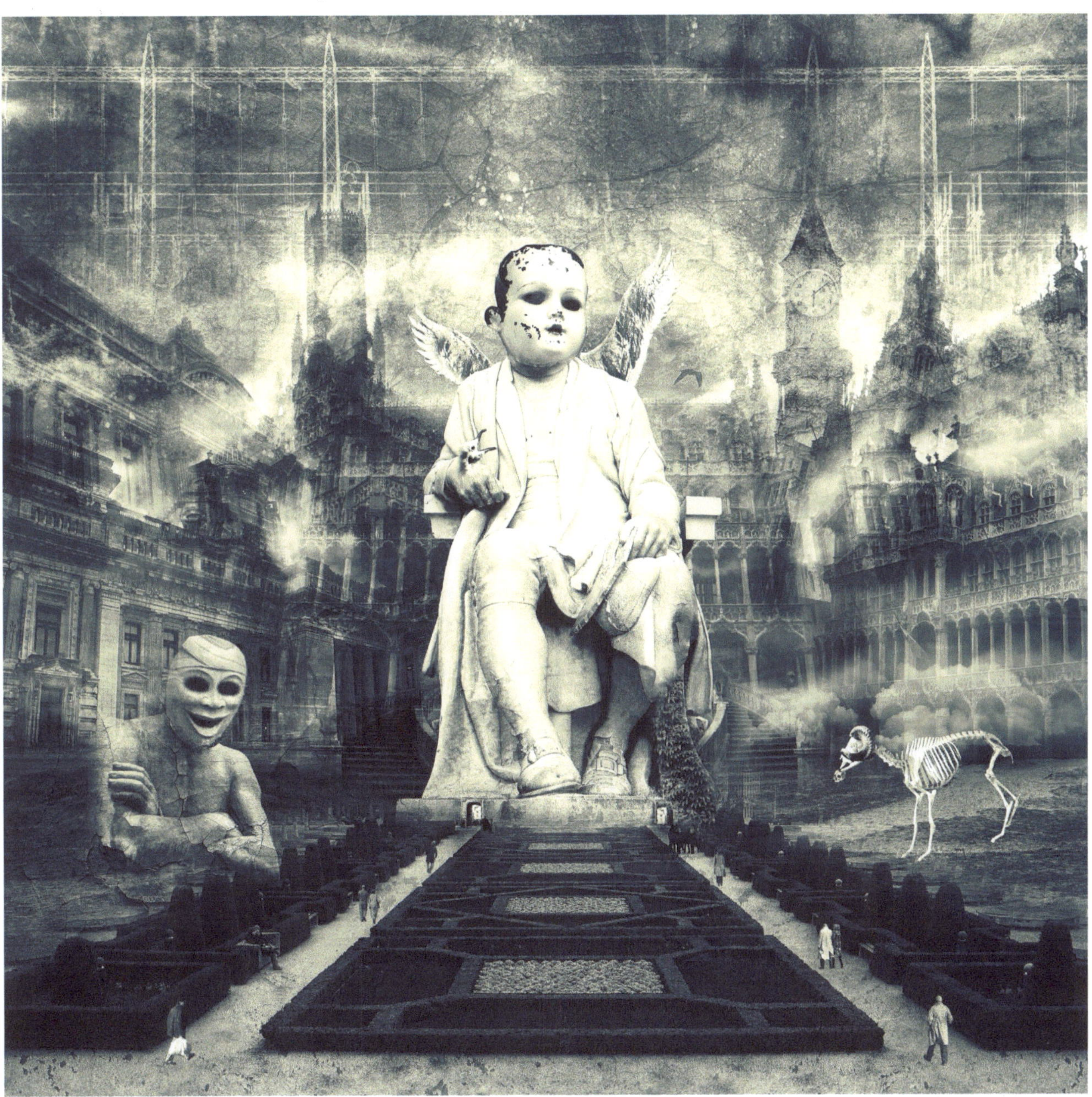

Prince of Dystopy, Marcin Owczarek, 2011, Courtesy Eyemazing Susan

this guy standing with his hands on his hips staring into the street. It was late afternoon on a Thursday, I had the day off and this guy—actually his profile, he was not directly facing me—snagged my attention. Approaching him, I looked to where he was staring—into the gutter at a pigeon pecking at a large hunk of French bread. And each time a car whizzed past, the bird would hop away and just avoid getting hit. The sculpture garden below my window contained concrete statues meant for a backyard or a grave; some of the pieces there were angels with downcast eyes and extended wings, others were massive urns. The pigeon, black yet splattered with gray a la Pollock, was scrawny and desperate-seeming and unwilling to abandon the hunk of bread, which was much too large for a bird to move. And this guy on Houston Street stood there staring at the pigeon, and then he made a slow move toward it and the pigeon, as if understanding, hopped up onto the sidewalk. The guy stepped into the street, picked up the hunk of bread and, bending slightly, gently dropped it onto the sidewalk right next to the pigeon, which immediately began to peck at his meal once again. The faces of the angels in the sculpture garden appeared rough and smooth at once, and their wings were always chipped, but somehow these flaws made them more beautiful. After a moment the guy became aware of me pausing there on the sidewalk watching him and he turned to look at me and I wish I could say that when he turned I was smiling but I wasn't and I wish I could say he appeared friendly but it was in fact the opposite of that. We just stood there looking at each other for the longest, most silent time and I saw this face that was rough like stone and his mouth that looked like both the meanest words and the sweetest could flow out from between his lips. His eyes, blue like the sky at the earliest hour of morning, looked vaguely cunning with those fierce black brows, and his nose was strong in his face and I could tell no matter what kind of work he did now, no matter where he lived, he probably came from a blue-collar mutt background like my own, and it wouldn't matter what clothes he had on—a tie showed above the zipper of his down coat, he wore good pants and cowboy boots—I would have recognized my type/his type. He scratched his forehead then and smiled, flashed a kind of barroom grin and I laughed outright and knew then and there I would never be able to help myself with him, I would always be a sucker for this guy with those eyes.

The sculpture garden below my window contained concrete statues meant for a backyard or a grave; some of the pieces there were angels with downcast eyes and extended wings, others were massive urns.

"You didn't see that." In the bitter chill his breath briefly unfurled in the air between us.

I shrugged, still smiling.

"I'm Tommy."

"Emily." Saying my name, I heard how my voice sounded high and thrilled and so different from his.

He stepped toward me and shook my hand and neither of us had gloves on and I felt calluses. His blue eyes, so like my mother's, surprised me with their warmth. Although I hesitated, shifting my book from hand to hand, shyly glancing beyond him at the passing foot traffic of this city, the constant motion of transient strangers who seemed to offer another gamble, a better chance for a better fit, a more perfect possibility for love, I said yes when he asked if I wanted to go get a drink. I sensed he wouldn't think less of me for so easily allowing him to pick me up there in the street. And no matter what was said later when we would fight, casual words tossed like Nintendo grenades into each other's psyches, my memory would always return to that afternoon near the knish place—to that moment when I watched him bestow such sweet kindness on some forlorn bird trying to survive one more day on an island made of schist.

Russian Graves

Larissa Shmailo

ONE OF MY FAVORITE PLACES IN THE world is the Russian Orthodox Cemetery in Spring Valley, New York, which is known as Novo Diveyevo. An Anglo, used to containing his dead in unrelenting grids of slabs of stone atop preternaturally manicured grasses, would have trouble envisioning it. For the Anglo, as Philippe Ariès has pointed out, cemeteries are frightening places that require control and taming. Hence, Anglos would be unprepared for the Slavic chaos at Novo Diveyevo, announced at first glance by the profusion and untrammeled growth of dogwood, maples, rose bushes, geraniums, wisteria, lilacs, spruces, marigolds and every other kind of plant imaginable. Like the death that is their ground soil, the plants grow everywhere, regardless of the boundaries of graves, the vehicle pathways or the buildings.

As for the graves, some are marked with simple wooden Orthodox crosses, the names long effaced by decades of weathering; some are huge marble monuments to heroes of the White army; atop one grave, one man built a small house with a bed and a chair and an embroidered rug for his extended visits to his wife (he doesn't come any more; this is probably not neglect, I think, but the fulfillment of his obvious consummate wish, reunion). I have always

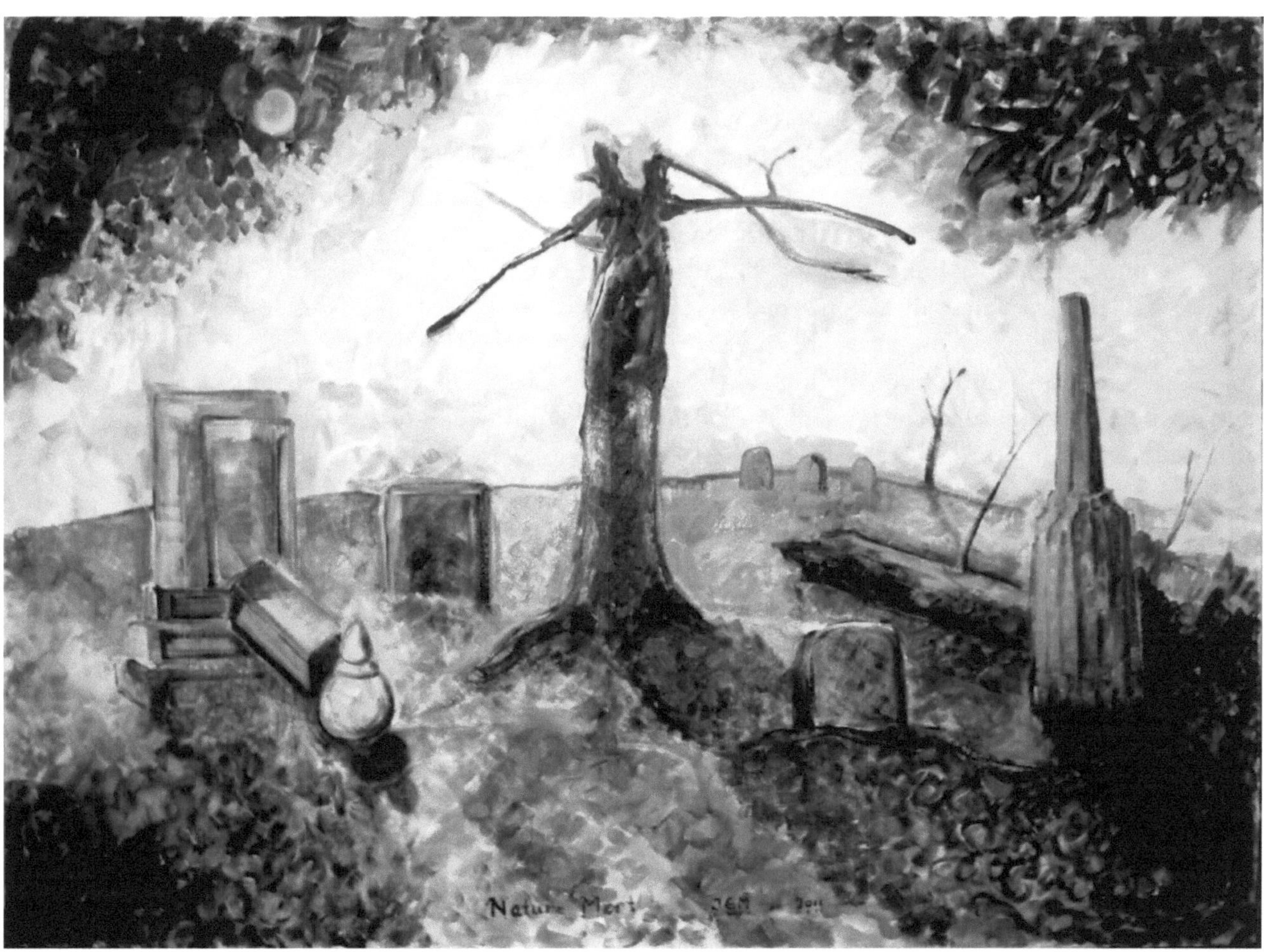

Lightning-Struck Tree in Cemetery, 60"x 45", oil on canvas, John Griffin

loved this small edifice and its promise of eternal love beneath the weeping willow that shelters its roof, as well as the imposing neighboring grave belonging to General Bezsmertnye, as its tall granite monument proclaims, a name which means, in translation, "immortal."

As the trees and uncut hedges grow as they please, so the graves are in lines or circles as they choose, and the wildlife goes about, oblivious of the black-frocked priests with their heavy iron crosses and the self-effacing nuns, the monashki, married to the priests. Raccoons lead their young across the small gravel driveway that serves as the entrance to Novo Diveyevo as the cars wait to park in the small places behind the church. Raccoons lead their young across the small gravel driveway that serves as the entrance to Novo Diveyevo as the cars wait to park in the small area behind the church. The church is mainly a site for funerals these days, with a dwindling congregation made smaller by every death. The current clientele of Nova Diveyevo is that greatest generation, veterans of the Second World War, and they arrive more frequently with every year of the new millennium.

Funeral masses are heavy with incense and read in Old Church Slavonic. There is crying, but little keening. Caskets are almost always open and we kiss the hands and the heads of our loved ones in parting, but feel a loss if, for some reason, we cannot. We feel comfort that we are putting our forefathers into the hands of the diligent nuns who will weed the graves and let us know if the gophers are eating holes under the plots and making them sag.

There is—and this is truly incomprehensible to the Protestant—an old age home on the premises; the monashki care for these aged. The place is free of the howling agonies of most age care facilities, where, as anyone who has ever been to one knows, the old lie screaming into the night, calling for their long-dead mothers. Here the old understand they are going to die and accept it, and are happy with the care of the meek monashki, so unlike the jaded, burnt-out nurses of clinical aseptic hospital wards, and with the physical beauty of the final resting place they have chosen.

I grew up with little fear of the dead. All my people—both sets of grandparents, and now both mother and father, other relatives—reside here and I take comfort in visiting them. When I was a child, before the cemetery grew large and woods—yes, even here—were cut down to make room for more dead, my father would take me walking by the woodland streams, showing me the small fish and salamanders in the rivulets and the mushrooms growing on the rotting carcasses of the old woodland giants. My mother would make a picnic. Camp survivors, they had learned to live, or at least make peace, with life and death both.

I said all my people were at Novo Diveyevo—not true. The most important of all, my godchild and niece (suicide? overdose?), chose to have her ashes scattered over the Long Island Sound. To me, a horror. How to visit? Where would be the lilacs and rabbits and raccoons to succor her, to succor me? Where, Lord, in that vast uncaring space they call the sea, would she be? My brilliant child, where are you? Damn you if you tell me she is in every sea breeze, in every mist, in the air I breathe. She is gone and yet I search for her as her molecules spread further and further away to the blank magnetosphere and into deeper space and finally into some accursed black hole. I have a brief with God: I demand habeus corpus.

At Novo Diveyevo, we could have talked, she and I, about this, about her death so unnaturally preceding mine. I could have bought a bench to plant next to the grave and, after many years, perhaps, we could have come to an understanding. If not understanding, then perhaps peace. But how does one come to terms with the sea? With the wind over the ocean? With ashes? With space?

I will do what I know how to do, what I have been taught. I will find a bench near that insatiable sea. I will look for the last molecules of my beloved. Maybe the gulls and terns and clams will take pity on me and guide me somehow to whatever is left of her whom I loved so.

New Paintings

John Lurie

John Lurie's drawings and paintings express a disarming mixture of corrosive wit, raw emotion and unblemished sensitivity. His works bear the mark of an outsider, a quality present throughout his idiosyncratic career. To quote the artist: "I like to draw and paint. It is a river to me. I am not an Indian."

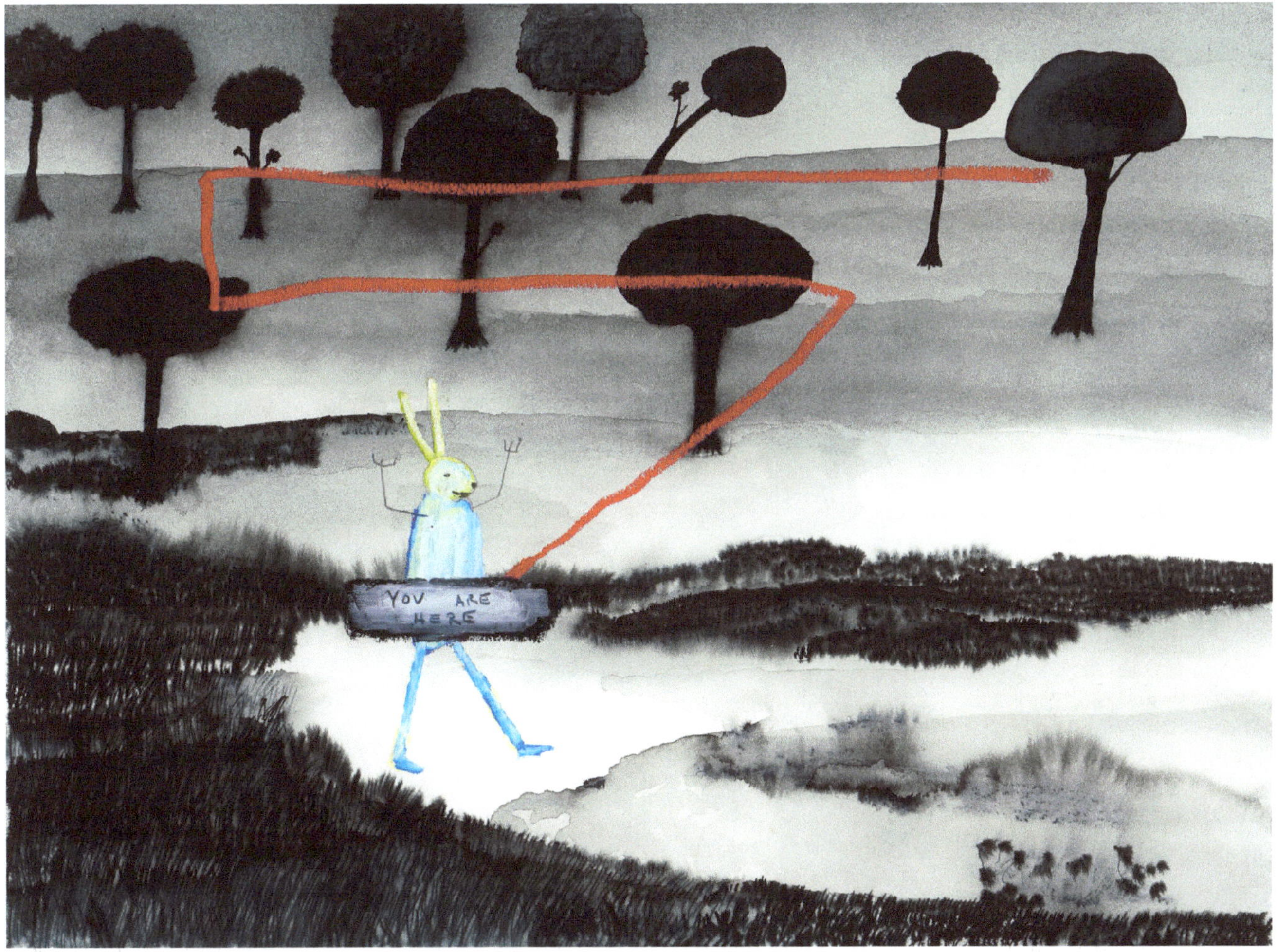

You Are Here, 12" x 9", ink, oil pastel and graphite on paper

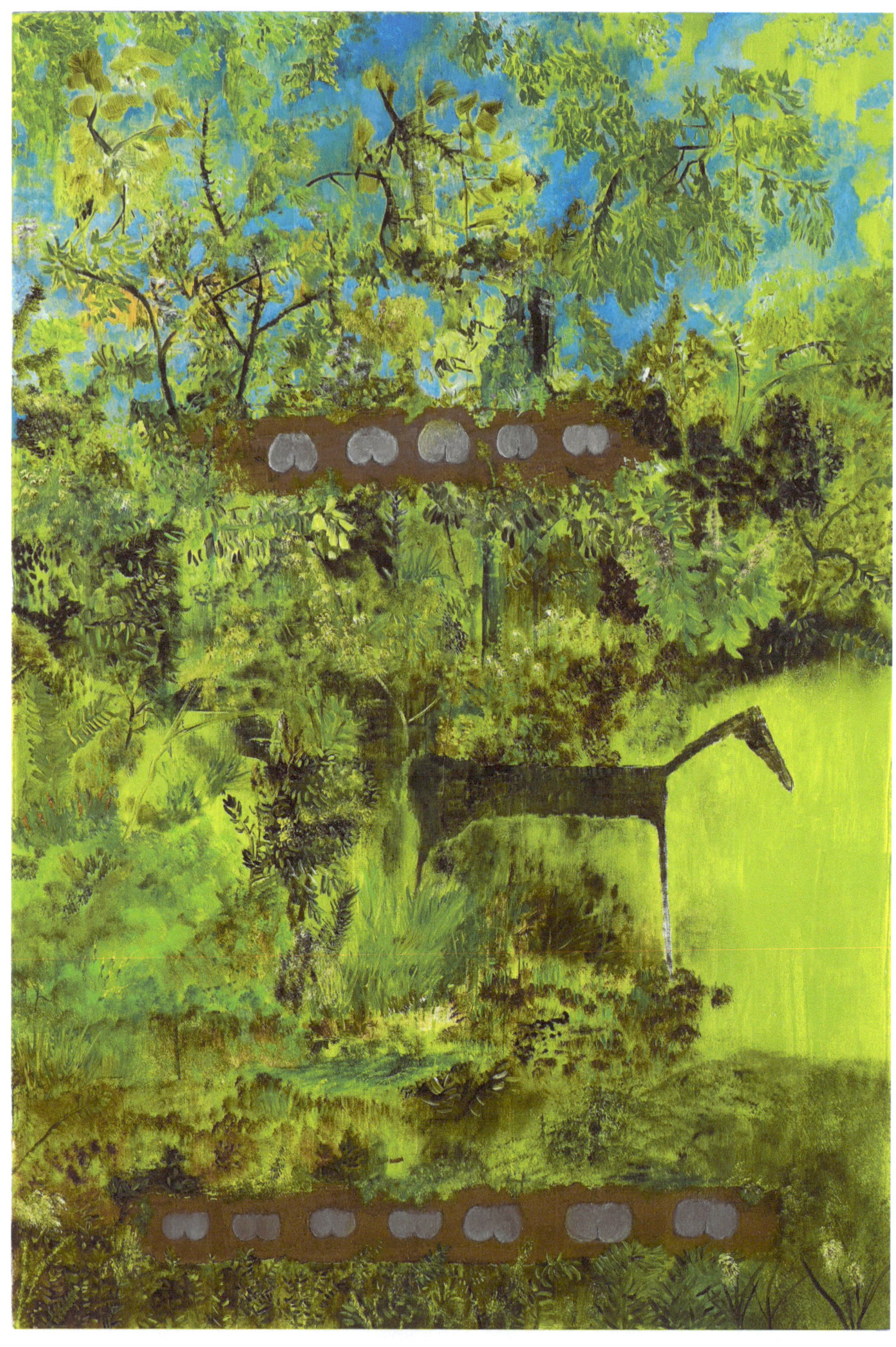

Twelve Bottoms Against Nature, 35"x16", oil on linen

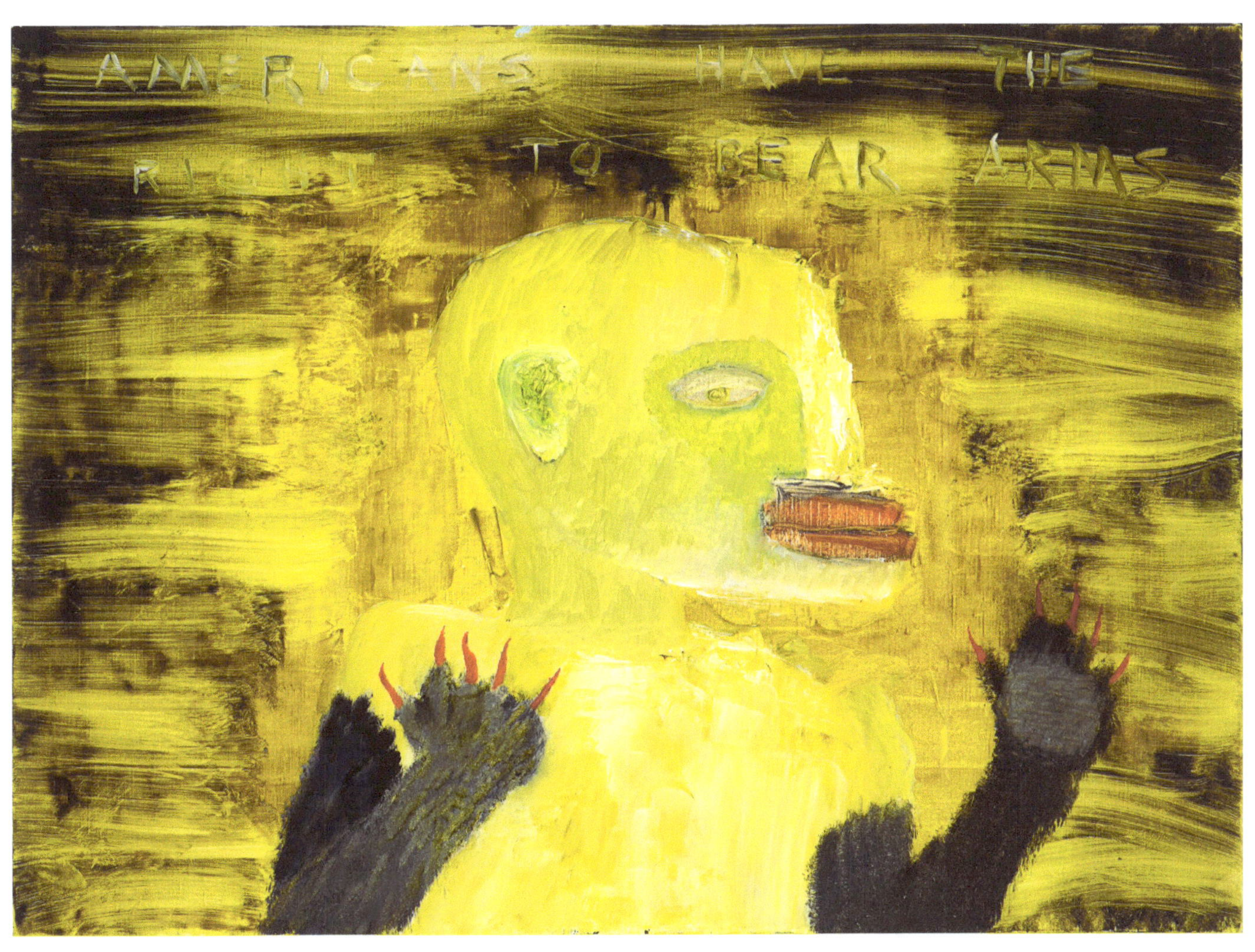

Americans Have the Right to Bear Arms, 18"x24", oil on linen

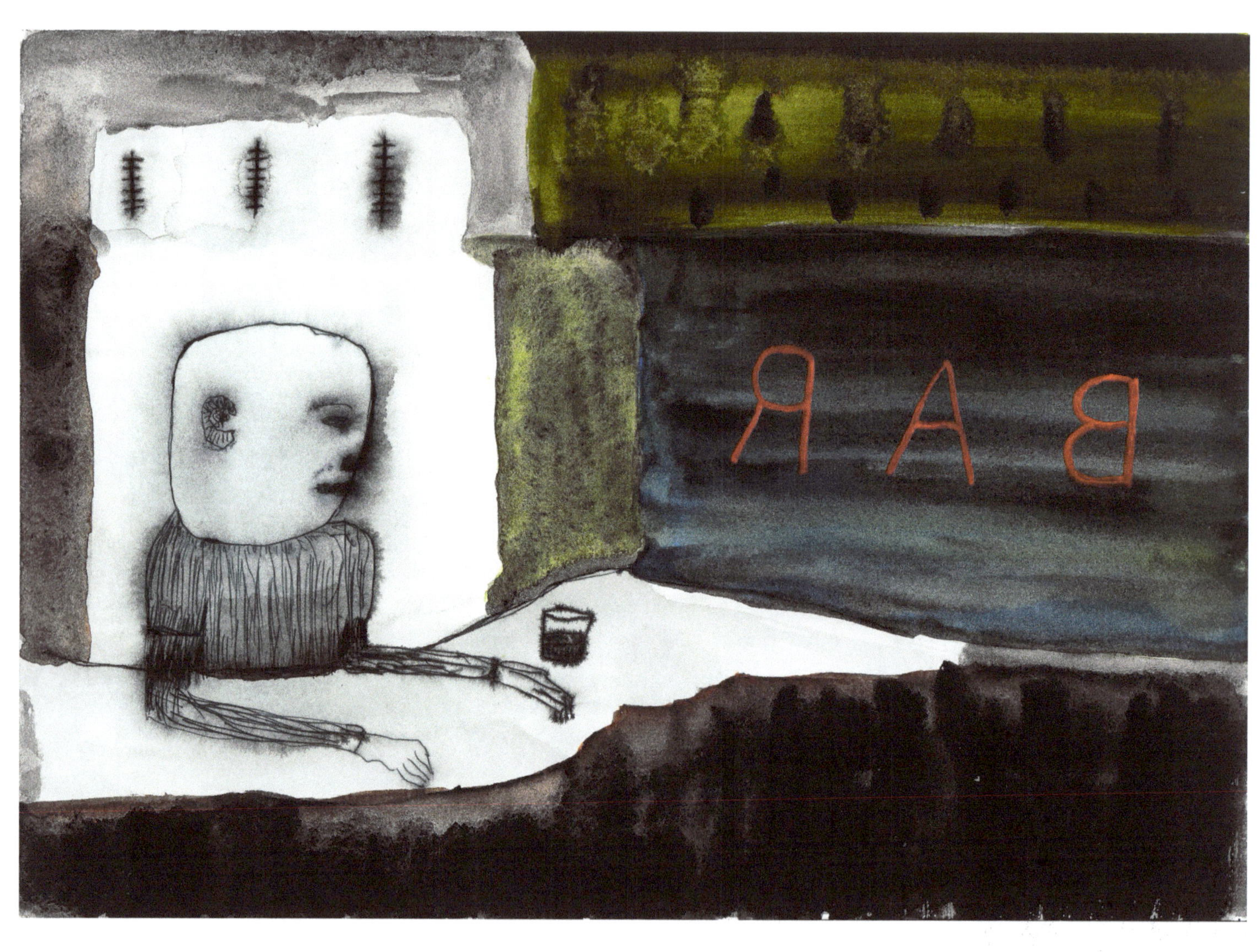

Bar, 14" x 10", watercolor,ink and oil pastel on paper

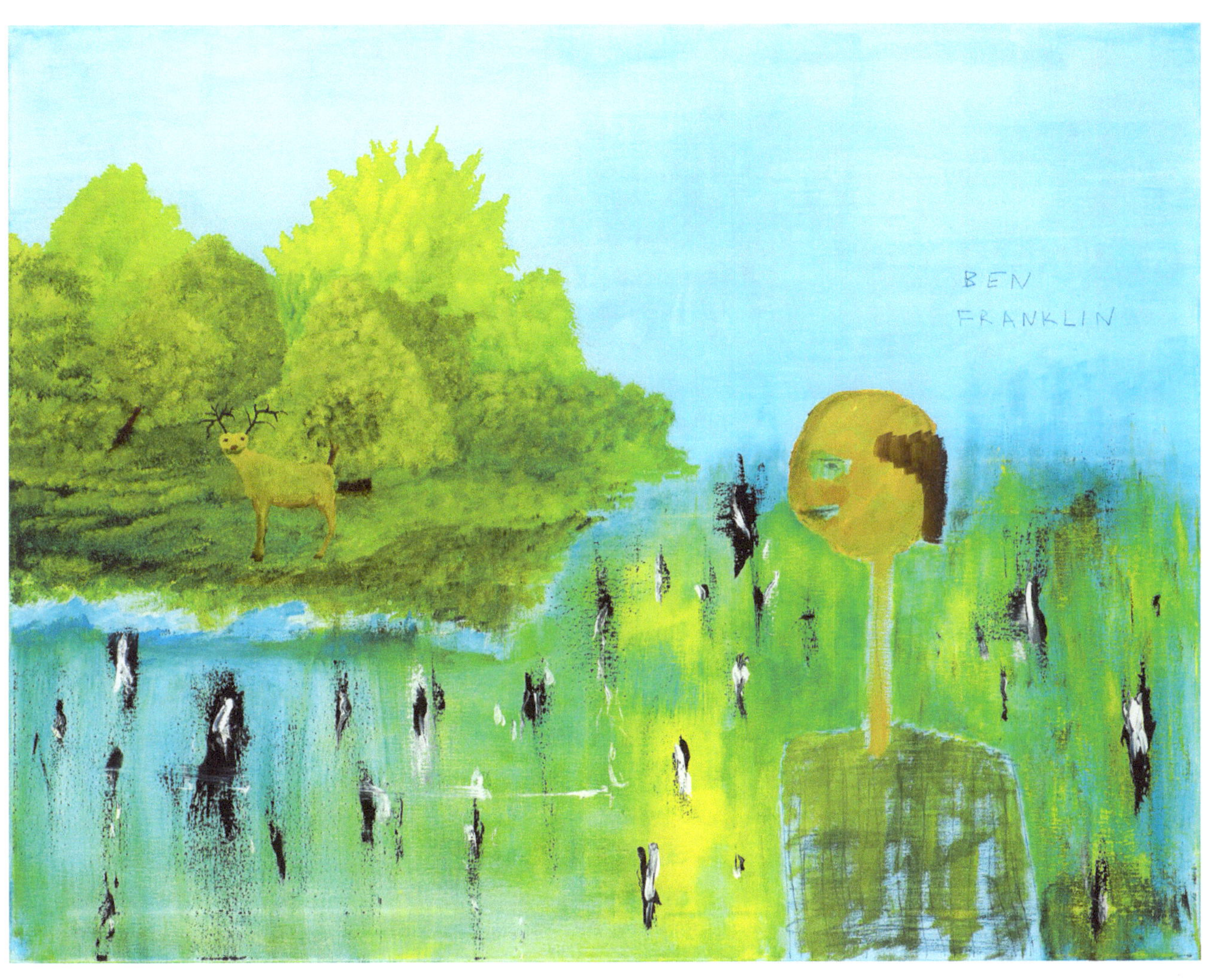

Ben Franklin, the Inventor of Trees, 36"x28", oil and graphite on canvas

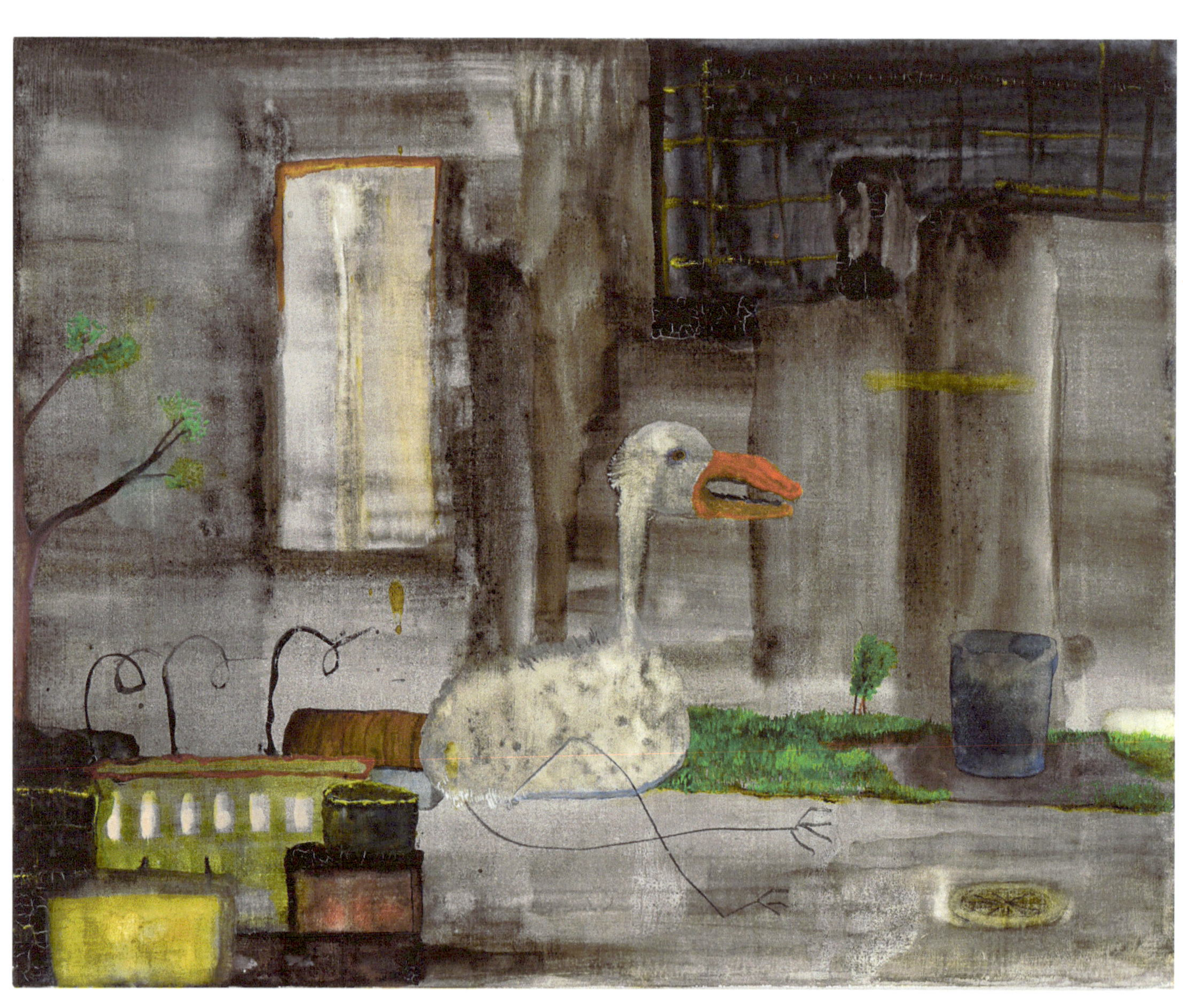

Bird Falls Near Chinese Garbage, 16"x20", watercolor and ink on canvas

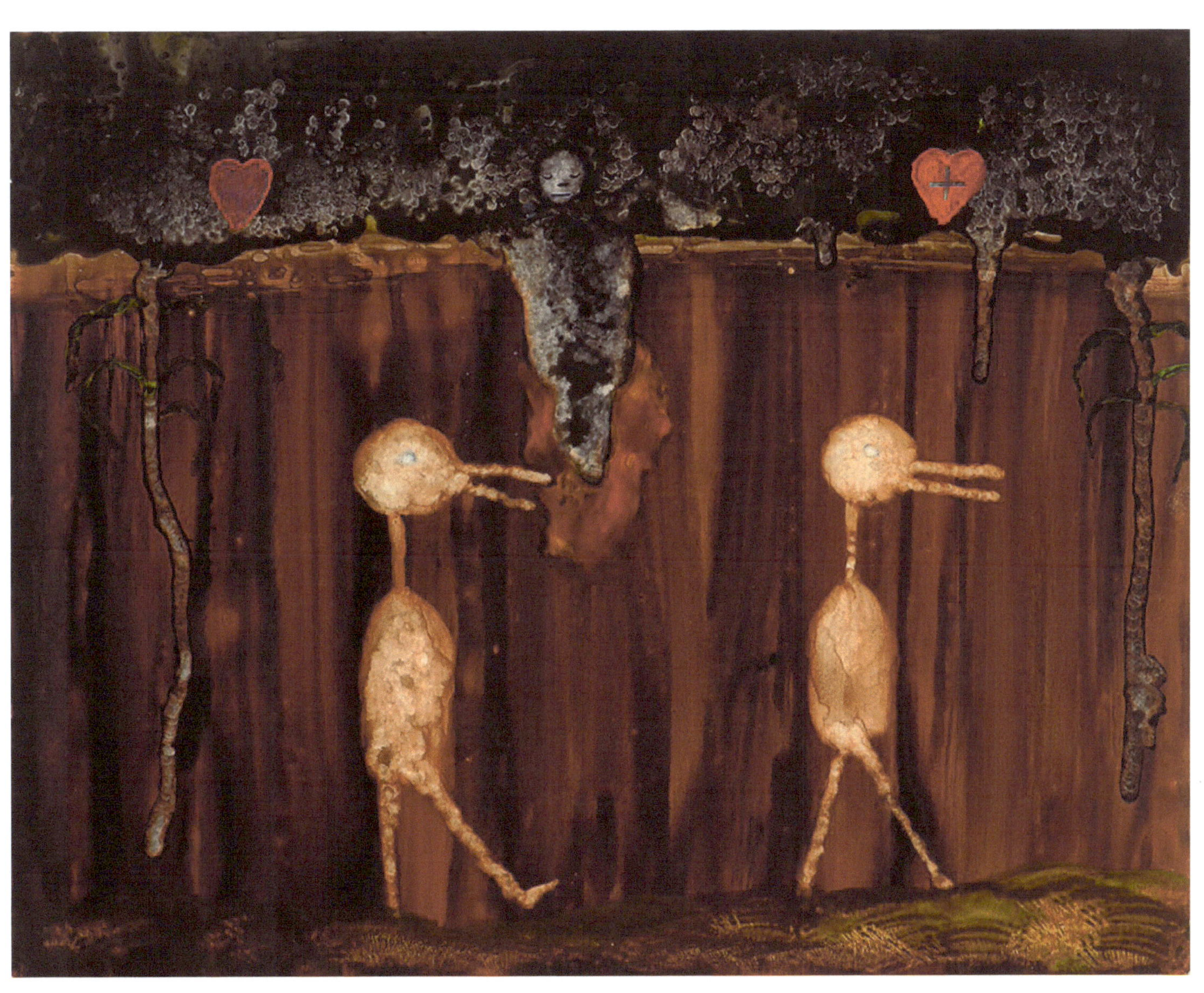

Birds of the Hideous Divine, 16"x20", watercolor, oil pastel and graphite on clayboard

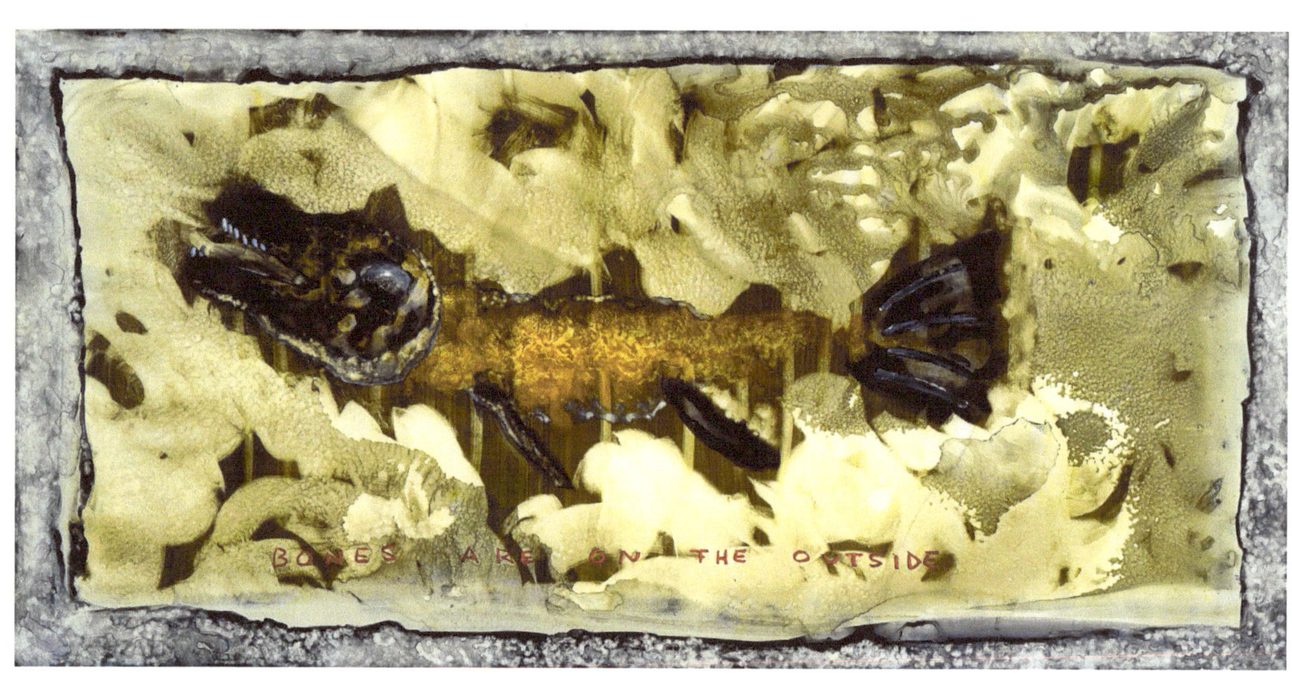

Bones Are on the Outside, 18"x36", watercolor and ink on clayboard

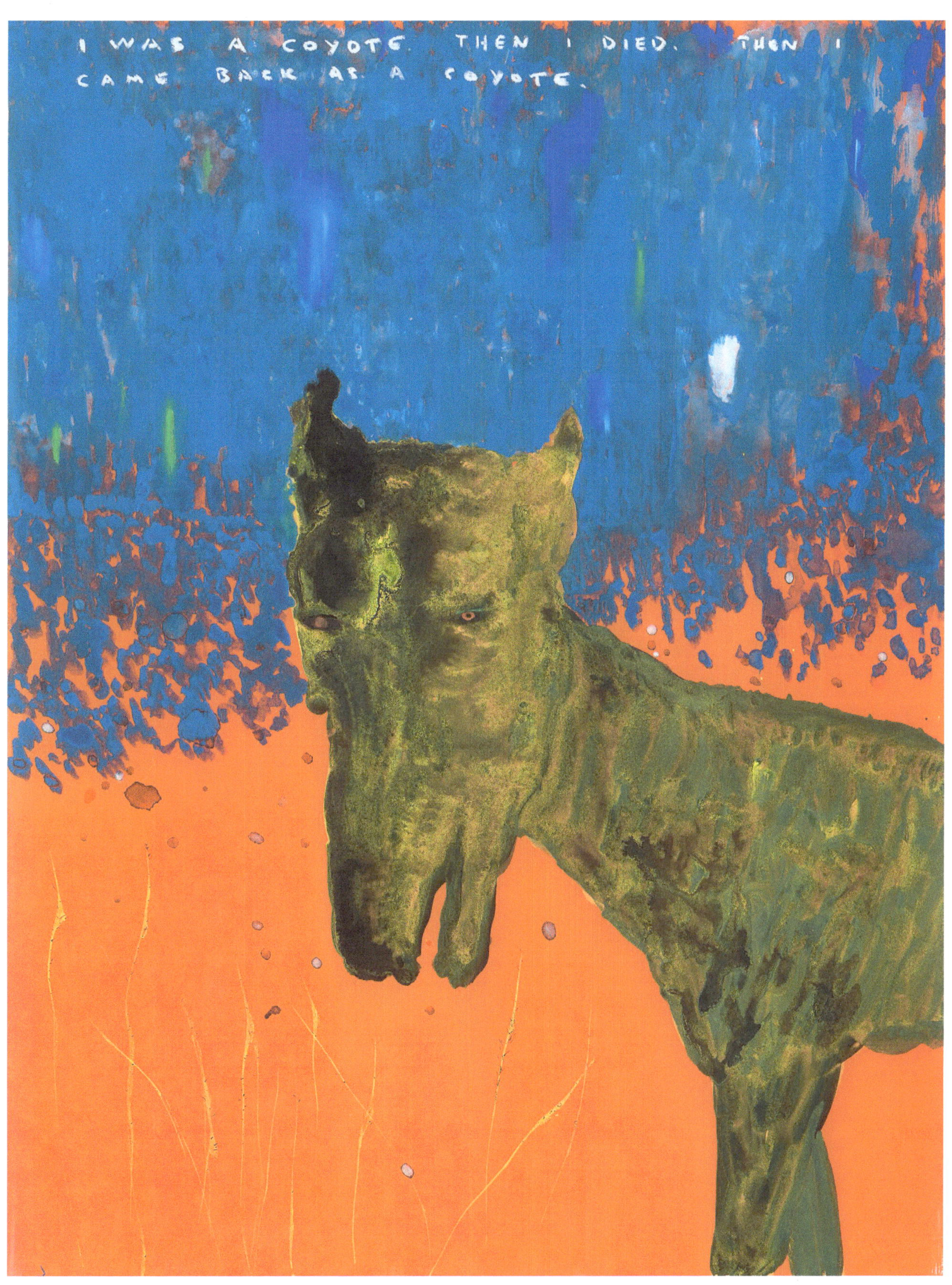

I Was a Coyote, Then I Died, Then I Came Back as a Coyote, 24"x18", watercolor, ink and oil pastel on paper

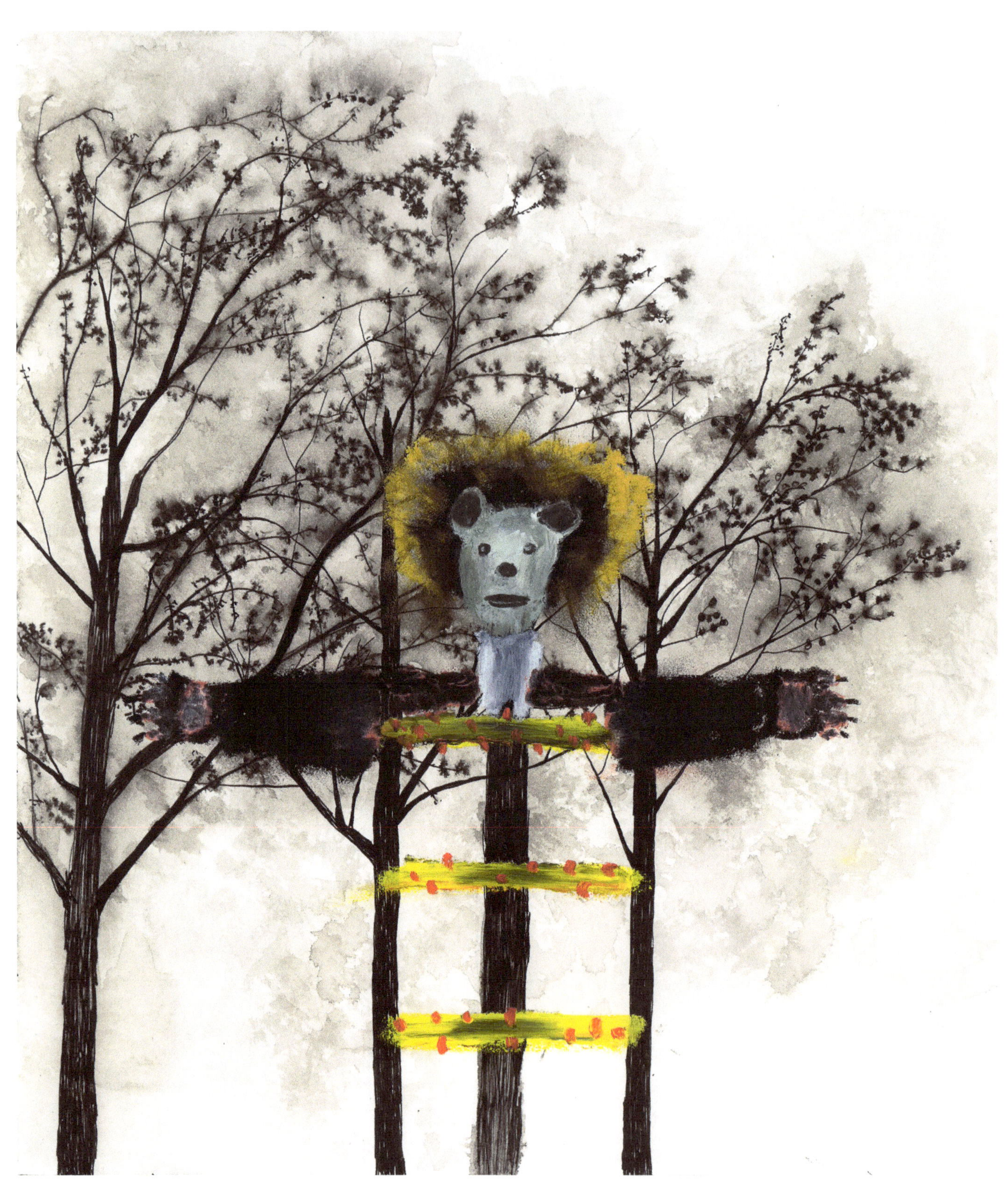

Give Up. Americans Have the Right to Bear Arms, 8"x10", ink and oil pastel on paper.

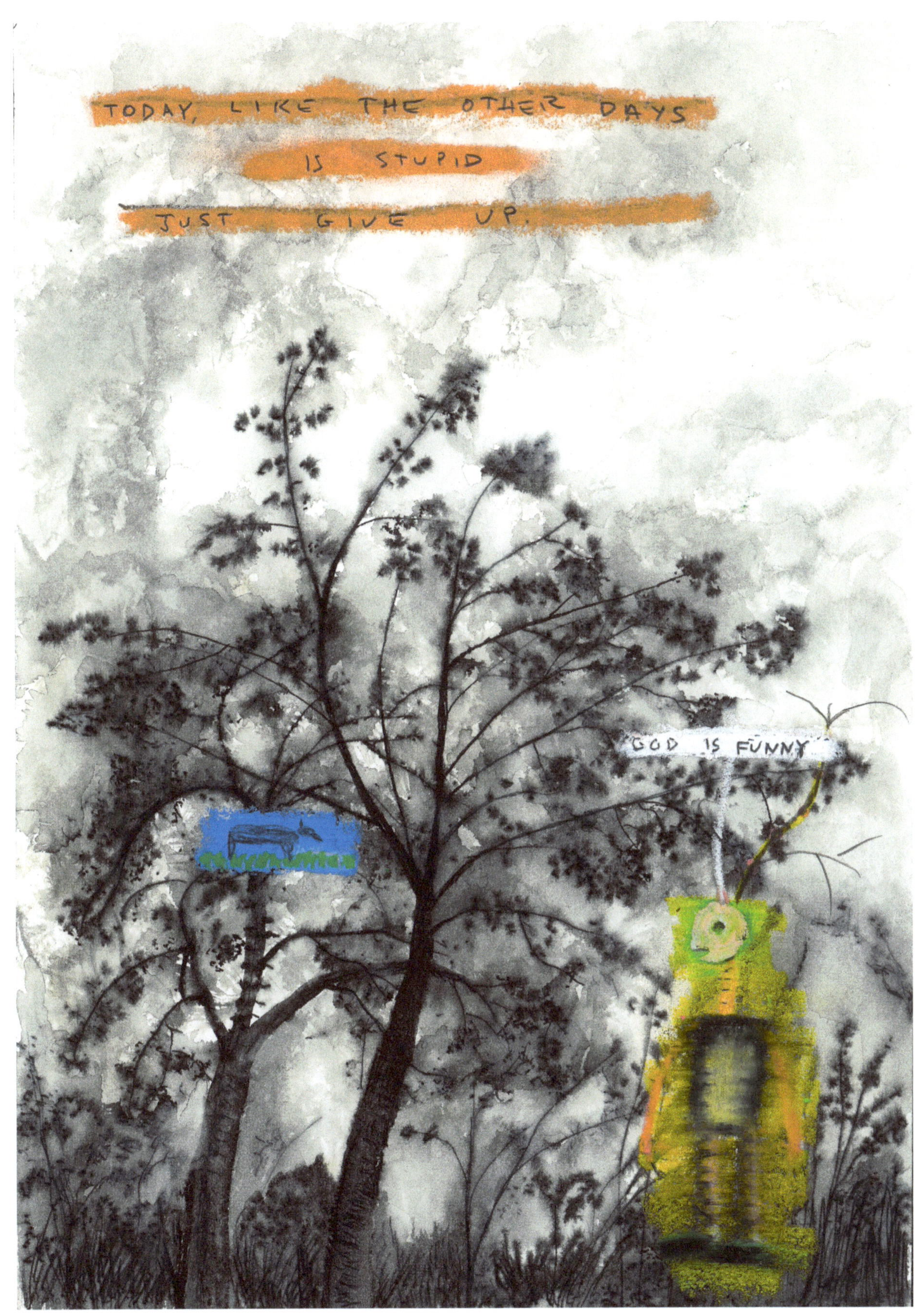

God Is Funny, 7"x10", ink and watercolor on paper

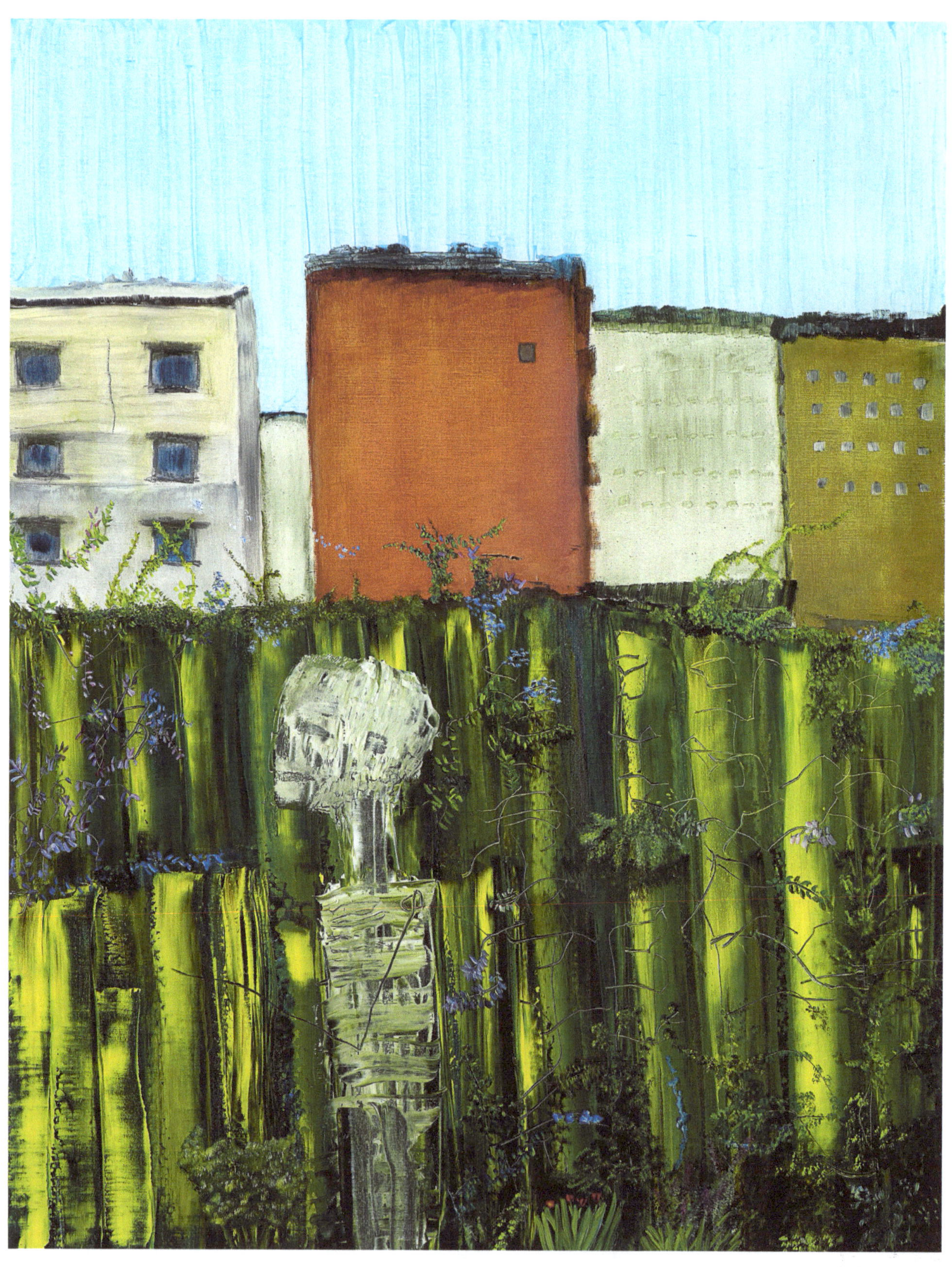

I Am Thankful for My Skeleton. He Is Out in the Garden, 26"x36", oil on linen.

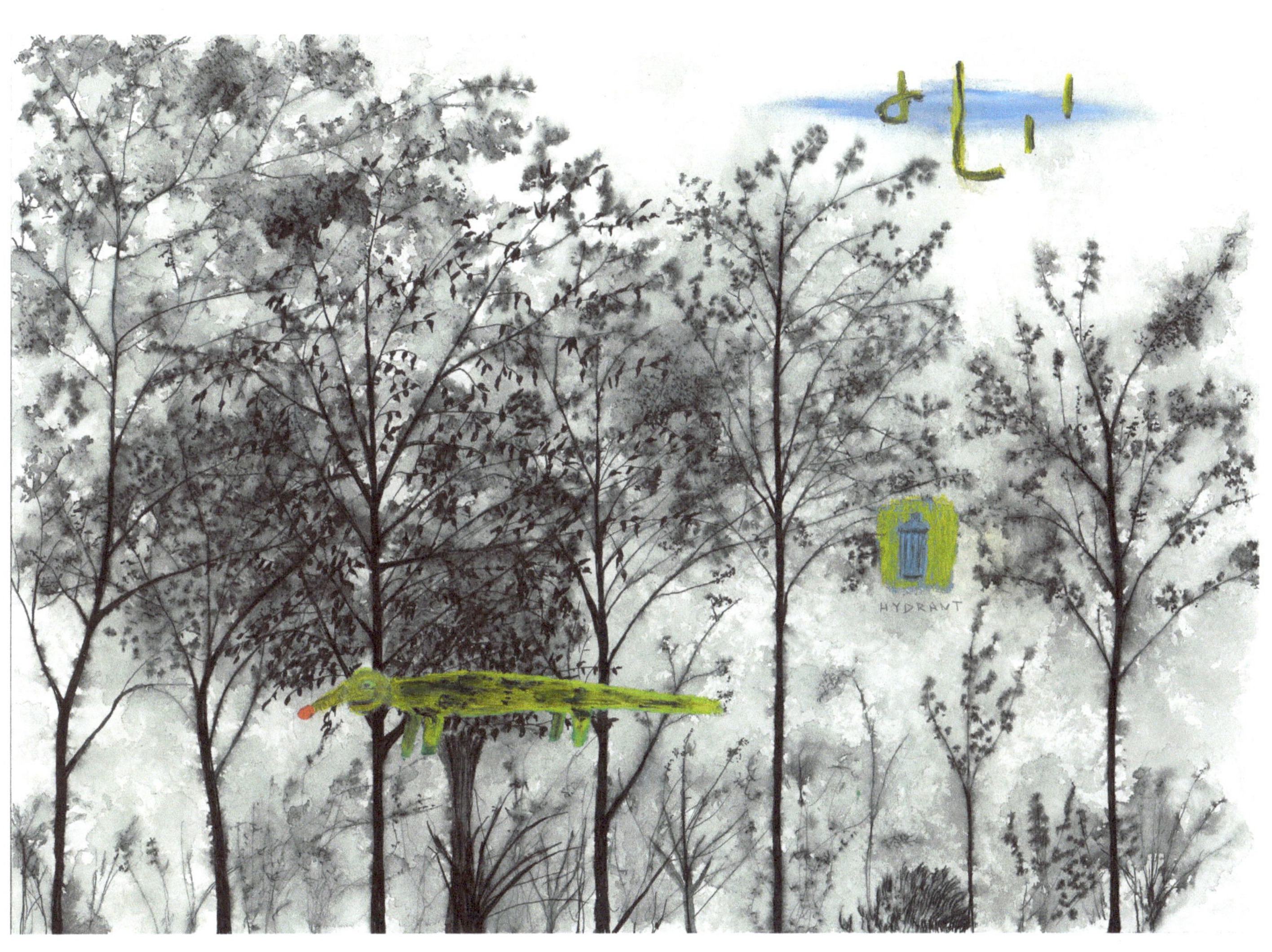

Honk Nosed Lizard and Hydrant, 10"x14", ink, watercolor and graphite on paper

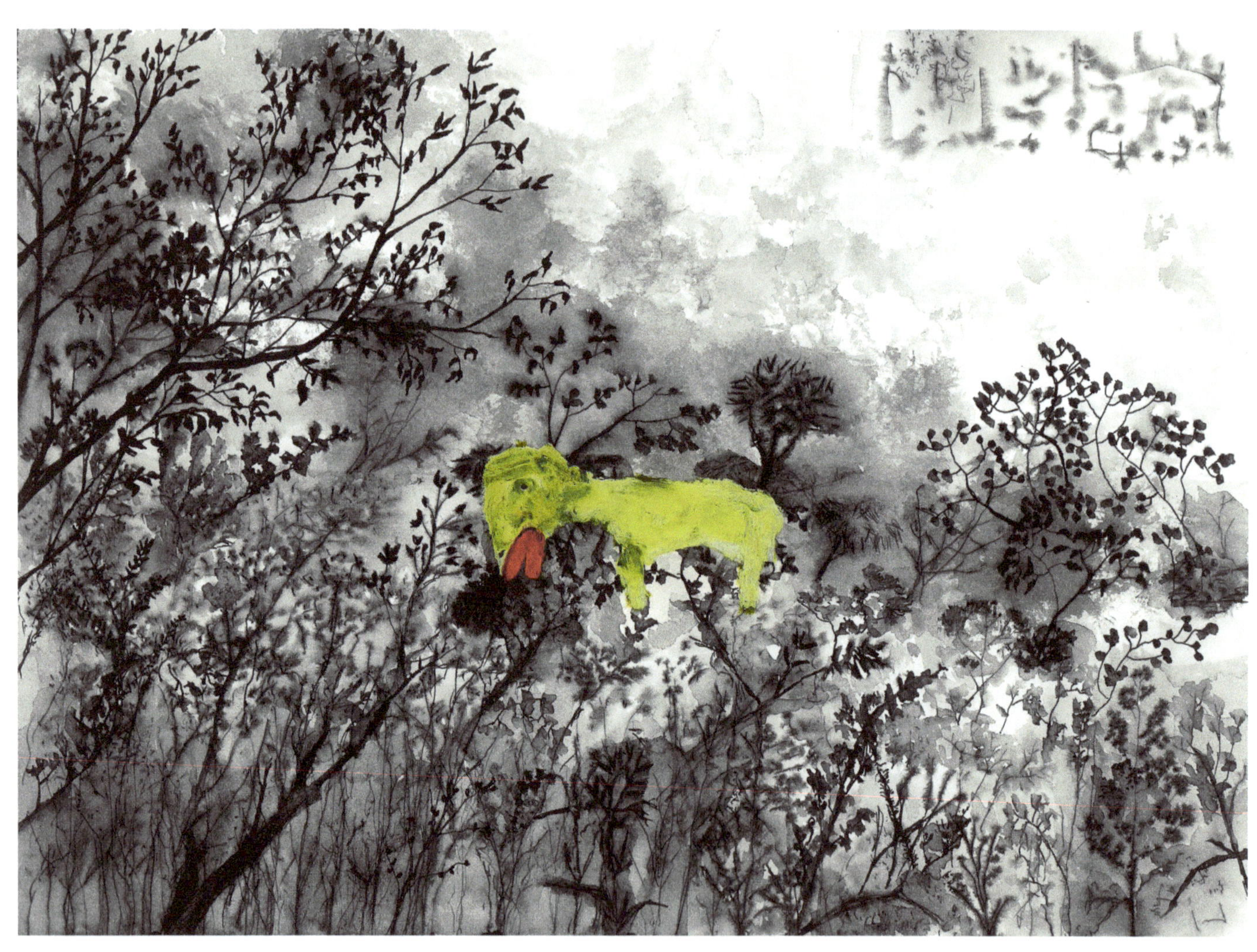

The Invention of Animals, 9"x12", ink and oil pastel on paper

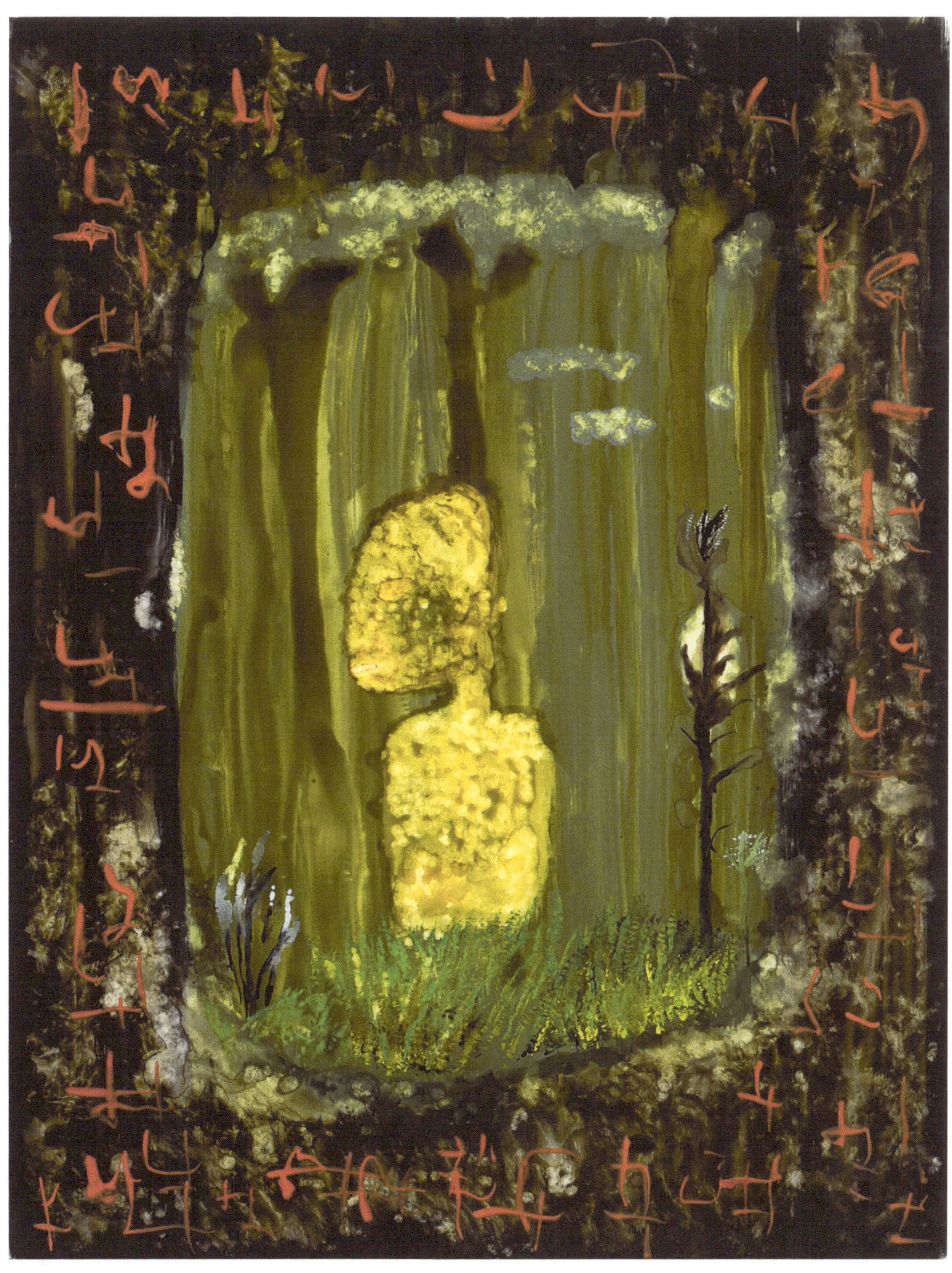

John and Jaya, 18"x24", watercolor and oil pastel on clayboard

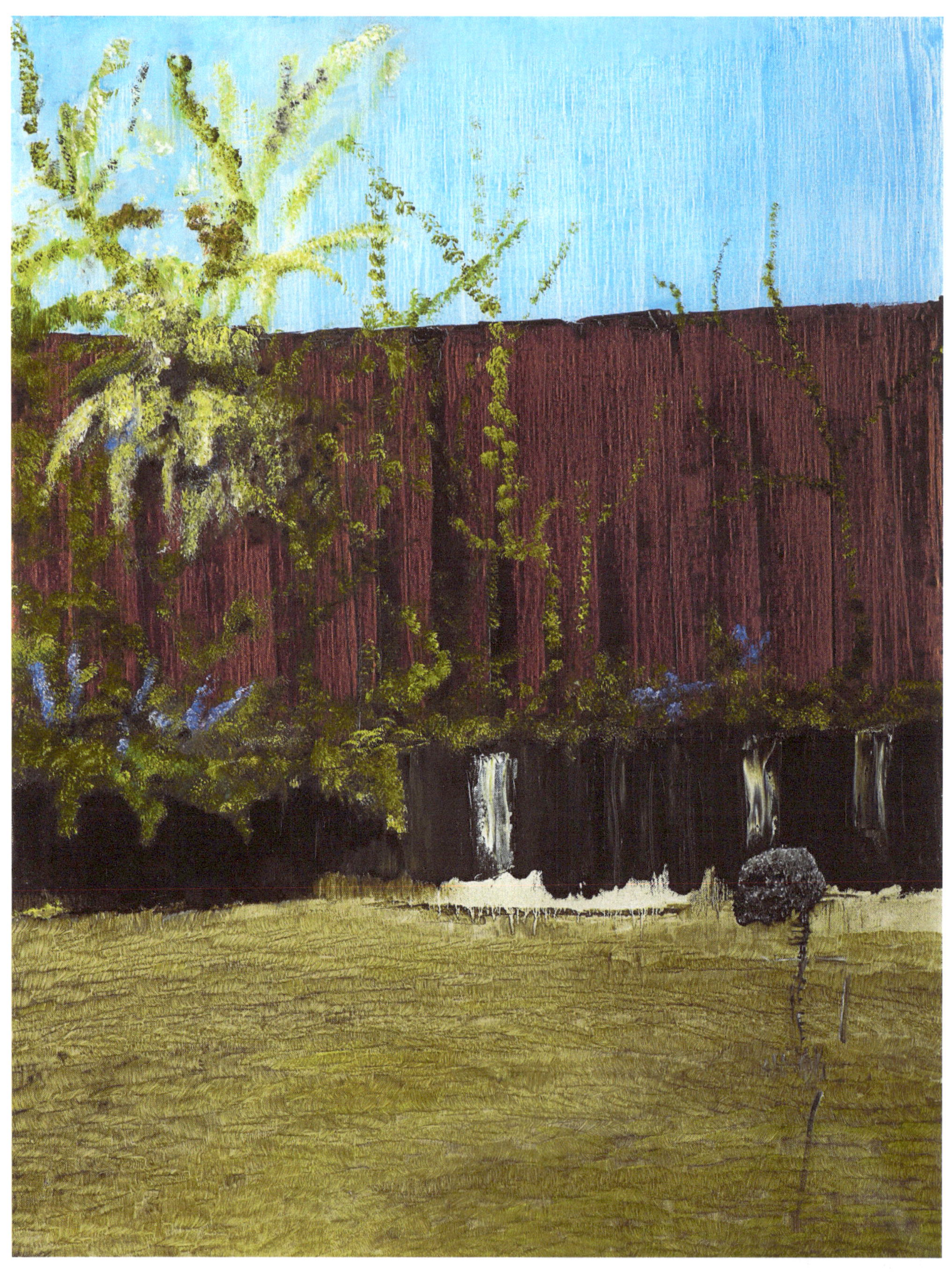

The Skeleton in My Closet Has Moved Back Out to the Garden, 18"x24", oil on linen

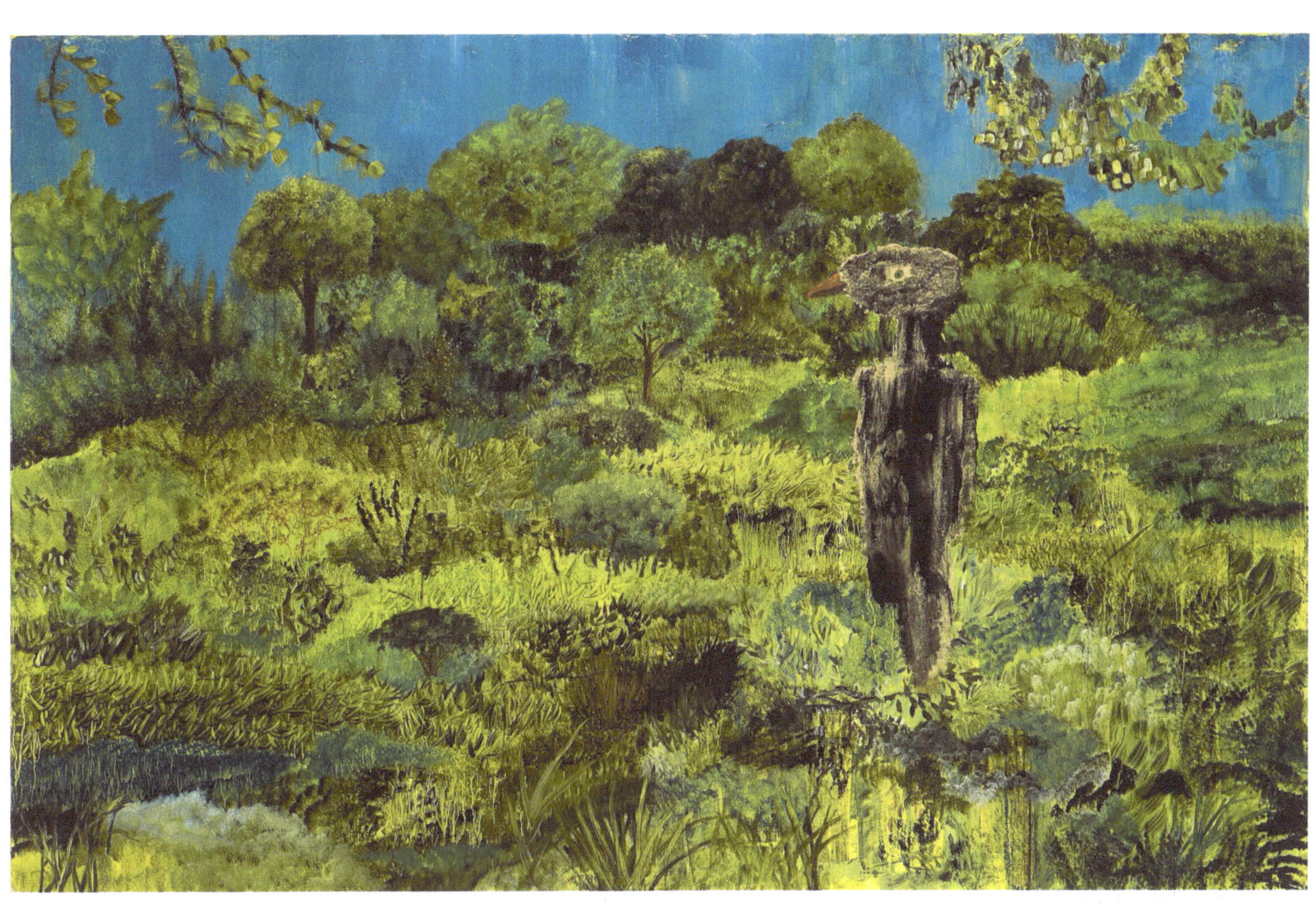

Man Cannot Destroy Nature. Nature Is Too Mean, 24"x36", oil on linen

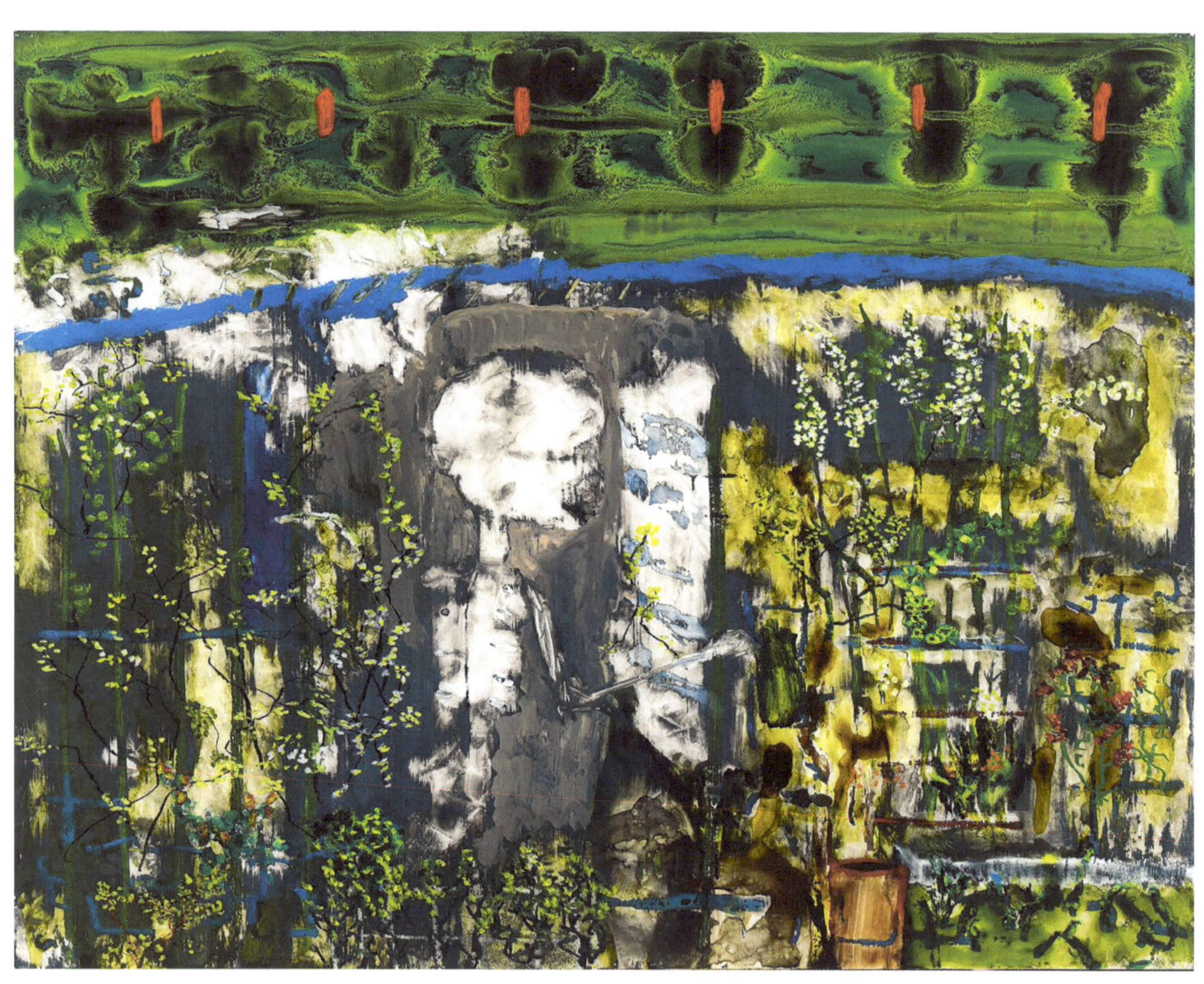

The Skeleton in My Closet Has Moved Out to the Garden, 16"x20", watercolor, oil pastel and graphite on clayboard

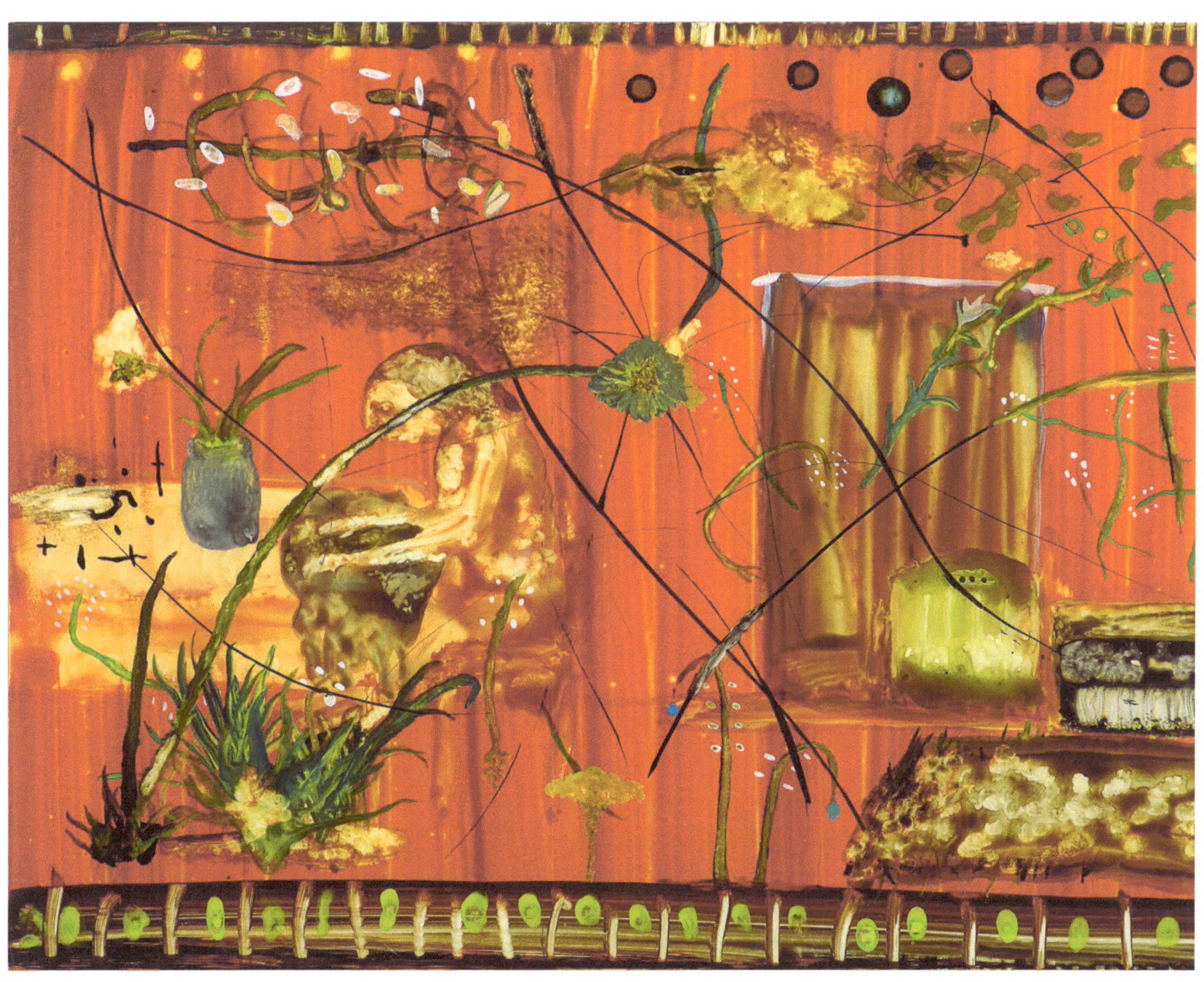

There Is a Caveman in My Apartment Examining the Fur. I Wish He Would Leave, 11"x14", watercolor on clayboard

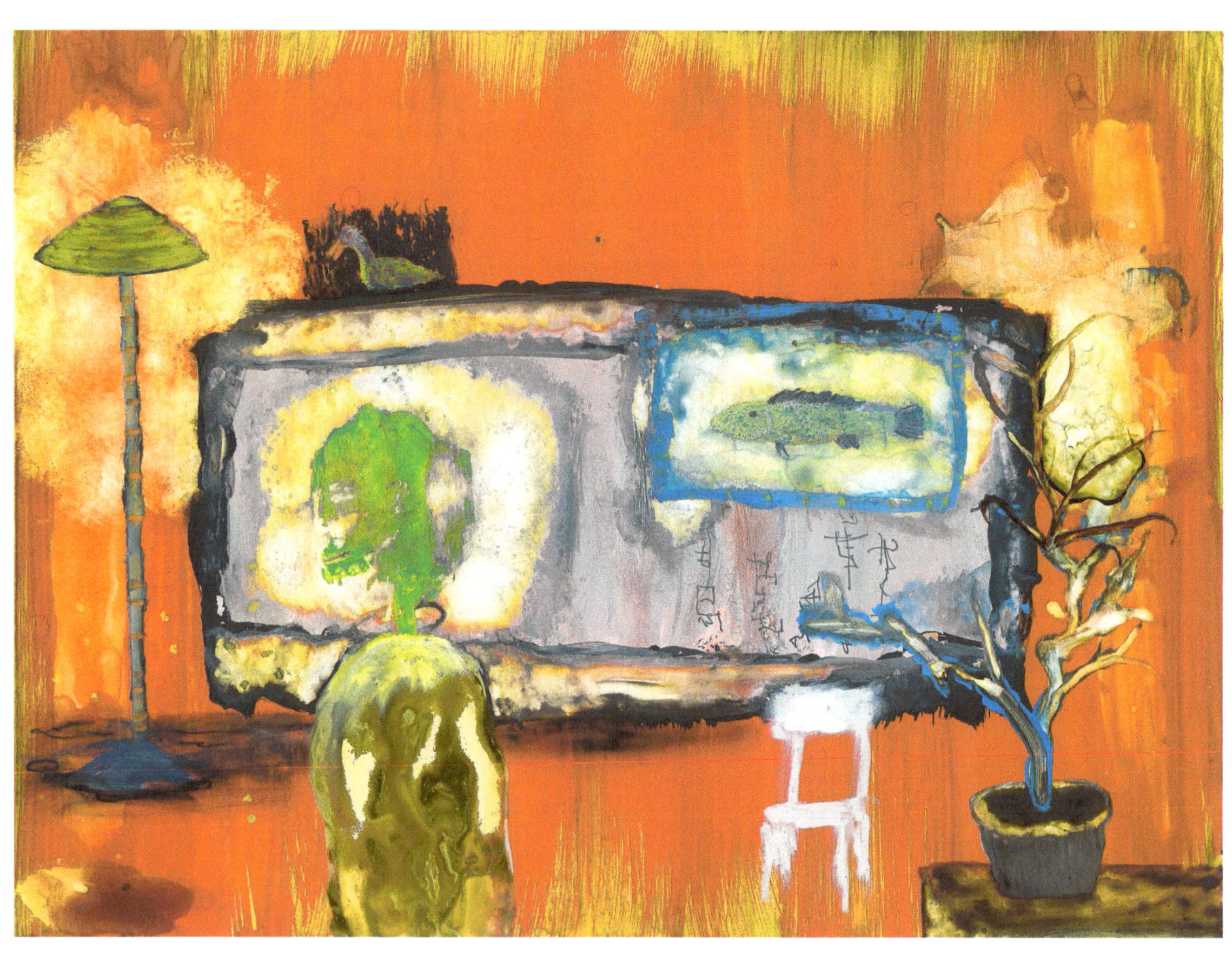

In This Painting the Artist's Soul Has Been Corroded by Assholism, 12"x16", watercolor, oil pastel and graphite on clayboard

Chapter 90

Samuel Delany

***Note**: Inadvertently, Chapter 90 was left out of the printed version of* Through the Valley of the Nest of Spiders. *Insert it on Page 956. What is now numbered Chapter 90 becomes 91; 91 becomes 92, and so on, through the final chapter, which should be 114 and not 113.*

—S.D.

* * *

Residents of Diamond Harbor—and Gilead—had more or less gotten used to the idea of an aging bachelor captain for the ferry to the mainland when Captain Ed took off his peaked cap and, holding it nervously, introduced himself to a lawyer a decade his junior from Savannah, a black woman named Holly, who stood at the rail, smiling, in a baggy blue sweater. Clouds had been hammered into irregular plates of lead and steel and heaped in the northern third of the sky. Some had begun to drift southeast and, between, you could see silver edging.

Ed and Holly went for coffee and sat by a drizzly window at Reba's Place. Three months later, they were married in a civil ceremony and moved into one of the new houses in the Gilead Settlement. They seemed happy enough. When Hannibal came back from graduate school, he stayed on the futon in their attic and occasionally worked with his older brother on the boat.

The new water conduit for the Settlement's north end was a major event in the island's development. A mainland plumbing company finished the work on Ed and Holly's house that had to be done by licensed plumbers. Still, loose ends had to be tied up—mostly a basement john that was all Ed's design and which the builders had warned him was probably not a good idea. Ed had gone ahead with it anyway.

Then he dropped by to ask Eric and Shit if they'd take a look to see if they could do something with it. "Ain't no water pressure at all down there. The thing just drips." So Shit put on his shoes (at Eric's insistence), picked up the tool box, with his thumb pulled the canvas strap up on his shoulder, and Eric hefted the sack forward with an adjustable wrench and fifteen pounds of small pipe in it, the acetylene torch, and a bar of solder with a resin core.

Outside under the hickories, they got into Ed's blocky jeep.

(Shit still thought cars imported from India looked funny. So did Eric. But Shit had to talk about it from the time they got in to the time they pulled up to the gravel in front of Ed's house—the turf hadn't yet been laid—and Ed was stonily silent.)

"You think you two can do anything?" Ed asked pretty much of Eric alone. In the basement they looked across the sawhorses and the cans of paint still standing about.

"Sure," Shit said. "You're on the new line."

Ed said, "Yeah. But it doesn't have the pressure it should—yet." (Within the last few years, they'd helped out on three or more dozen prefab buildings within six hundred yards of Ed's. Whenever they had run into Holly outside, she'd been pleasant, with smiles and hellos and good mornings, but Ed—who rose before sunrise anyway, so that five out of six days they didn't see him—had never given more than a grunt to either handyman.)

"We'll see," Shit said.

"I gotta get back to the boat," Ed said curtly. "It ain't like when Jay and Mex did the runs. Wasn't nobody out here then. Half the time, they must have made their trips with nobody on the scow. Now people get upset it you're ten minutes late. Holly'll be home in a couple of hours."

The solution turned out to be going over to sift through the debris of two abandoned construction sites. Shit thought he remembered seeing one the last time they were over there: a fifty-gallon, plastic-lined

Mertle-Tubman canister, which they carried back between them. They set it up in the maintenance shack out back of Ed's, at ground level, right behind the john, and Eric made a stopcock from an old toilet mechanism. Pipes went from the kitchen line to the canister, then from the canister down to the cellar.

"You see," Eric finished explaining to Holly when she got home from her office near the docks (since Shit, while he could make things, often with great skill, was not good at describing how they worked), "when nobody's using the water up here, the canister fills out back, and you have about fifty gallons of pressure pushing water down to the basement. As long as you don't flush the basement commode more than three times in an hour, you'll have pressure down there."

"That's wonderful," Holly said. "I don't think we'll be using the basement commode that much."

"It'll do most of its fillin' when you ain't usin' the upstairs water," Shit said for the third time—only now, with Eric's added explanation, it made more sense—and Holly, in her blue jumper with the cutaway neckline and her matching blue skullcap, at least *looked* like she understood.

"Ed won't be back till this evening. How much do we owe you for this?"

"Well, I'll tell you"—Shit rubbed behind his ear—"the parts come free. *We* didn't have to pay for 'em; ain't no reason *you* should. Besides, Jay MacAmon always thought a great deal of your feller, there, Ed. That's why he worked so hard to make sure he got the boat run. But Ed's still on the Chamber of Commerce payroll, and while they got great benefits, they don't pay diddly-squat."

"We worked for the Chamber of Commerce twenty-five years over in the Harbor, so we know what we're talkin' about," Eric added, having figured out where this was going. "A lot of people were

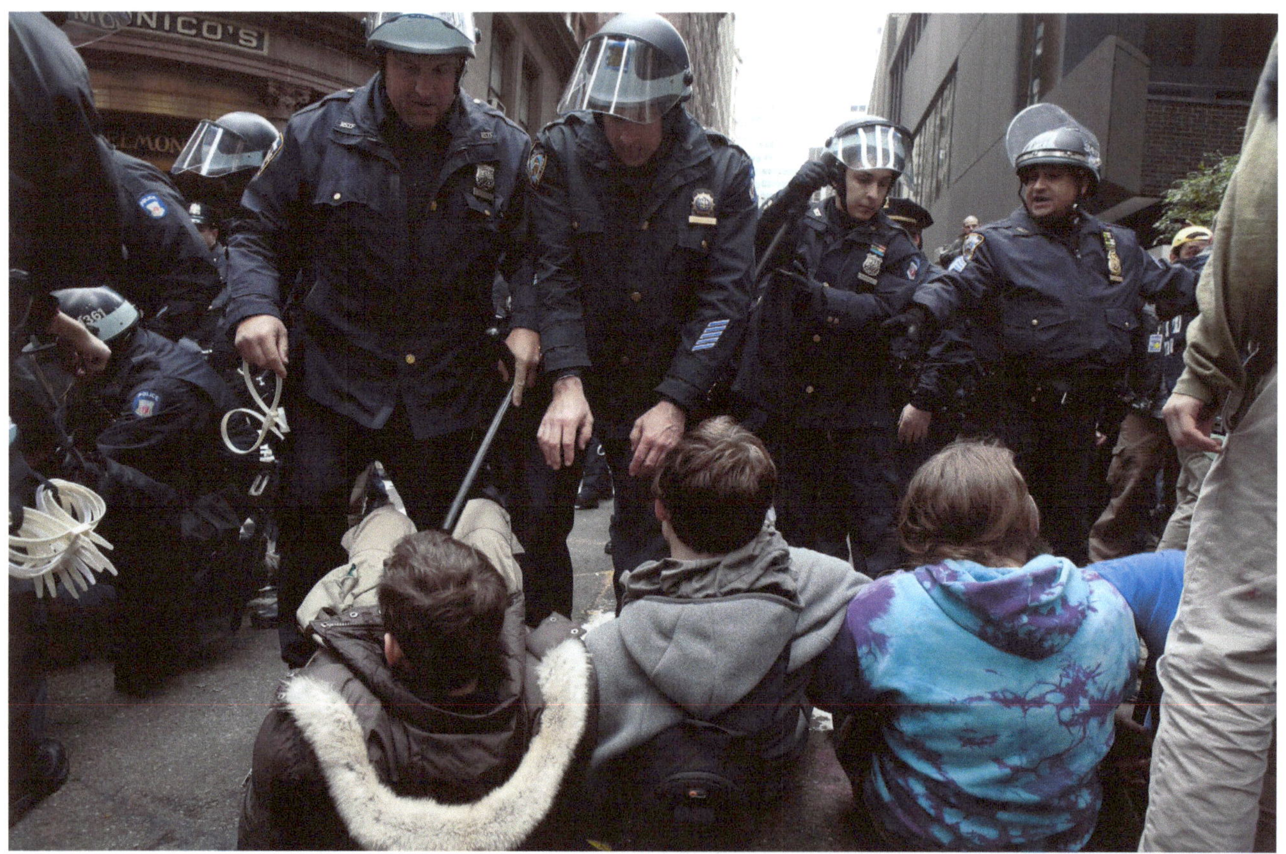

photograph by Ted Barron

awfully good to us, when we were coming up, people like Jay. So we ain't gonna take your money. And if you ever got any handy work again, you call us; we'll come do it. Your law office does all that pro bono work stuff, so you ain't makin' nothin' either. Other than for parts, you can tell Ed that, unless they cost us out of pocket, we ain't takin' a dollar from you."

Holly looked flustered. "Are you *sure*? I mean . . . well, that's . . . *more* than nice!"

"There're enough people in the Settlement here who pay us pretty well for what we do. Ain't no reason to take it from people who don't have it and are busy makin' things right for everybody else. That's what *he* done taught me"—Shit scowled at Eric—"and I just about got it learned."

"That's . . . well, that's an impressive philosophy."

Shit scowled at Eric even harder—because of the word, Eric realized.

Eric looked at the neatly dressed black woman, who stood, all but nonplussed, in her front foyer. As they started for the door, Holly asked suddenly: "Does that come from out of that philosophy book everybody says you're always reading?"

Eric stopped. He looked surprised. "I don't know." He shrugged. "I mean, maybe a little of it does; yeah, sure, some. But most of it comes from Jay MacAmon. And maybe Mr. Kyle. I mean, he gave Ed his job, he gave us our house. That's how you treat your family—"

"Even if they ain't sure they wanna be in your family, when all is said and done." Shit grinned slyly. "That's what his book says that he's always readin'. But you don't have to tell Ed that. Yeah, that's what Jay would've wanted. So that's what we're gonna do. You or Ed come over again, when you need somethin'. We'll see to gettin' it done, ma'am."

They left to walk through the mild winter, back around the Settlement toward the Bluff, past the Kyle mansion where scaffolding rose over two of its sides for the building's renovation into the Settlement Library, slanted shadows cutting tan walls into pale rhomboids, and ambled down the tufted path to their cabin.

They left to walk through the mild winter, back around the Settlement toward the Bluff, past the Kyle mansion where scaffolding rose over two of its sides for the building's renovation into the Settlement Library, slanted shadows cutting tan walls into pale rhomboids, and ambled down the tufted path to their cabin.

And every few months, they changed a light switch or puttied a loose pane or looked at what Holly had thought was a leak and explained it was only a pipe sweating at the joint.

After a dozen-and-a-half such jobs over a half -dozen years, one day Ed came by to say thank you for something. As he was leaving, with a hand on the screen door's metal frame, he stopped.

Shit said, "You want a cup of coffee, there, Ed? Before you go back home?"

"Thank you, Mr. Haskell—no thanks." One boot on the step below, he stood with the door open behind him. "You know, Mr. Davis—Mama Grace Davis—was right. You're a crude old man. You're *two* crude old men, but you're good people. That's what's important."

Then he was gone.

The screen door swung quick, till the ancient air stopper at the top slowed it, so that it settled closed: a quiet click. "How come it took him so long"—Shit came back from the counter to the kitchen table with his mug—"to figure *that* one out?"

Mayakovsky 1913: New Translations

Jenny Wade

Маяковский в 1913 году

Я тебя в твоей не знала славе,
Помню только бурный твой рассвет,
Но, быть может, я сегодня вправе
Вспомнить день тех отдаленных лет.
Как в стихах твоих крепчали звуки,
Новые роились голоса...
Не ленились молодые руки,
Грозные ты возводил леса.
Всё, чего касался ты, казалось
Не таким, как было до тех пор,
То, что разрушал ты, — разрушалось,
В каждом слове бился приговор.
Одинок и часто недоволен,
С нетерпеньем торопил судьбу,
Знал, что скоро выйдешь весел, волен
На свою великую борьбу.
И уже отзывный гул прилива
Слышался, когда ты нам читал,
Дождь косил свои глаза гневливо,
С городом ты в буйный спор вступал.
И еще не слышанное имя
Молнией влетело в душный зал,
Чтобы ныне, всей страной хранимо,
Зазвучать, как боевой сигнал.

Анна Ахматова—10 марта 1940

Mayakovsky in 1913

I didn't know you when you were in your full glory,
I only saw your fiery ascent,
But, maybe, today I have the right
To remember that day from years ago.
How sounds braced the lines of your poetry
With voices like we'd never heard…
Your young hands didn't rest,
And the scaffold you built was terrifying.
Everything you touched
Seemed transformed,
Whatever you wanted to destroy—collapsed,
A life or death sentence in every word.
Alone and never satisfied,
You tried to rush fate along.
You had already freely and willingly accepted
That soon you'd have to go out and join the great struggle.
I can still hear the answering roar
When you read to us,
The rain slanted its angry eyes,
You started a wild fight with the city.
And your still-unknown name,
Flew into the stuffy lecture hall like lightning,
So that today, cherished everywhere in this country,
It could ring out like a battle cry.

Anna Akhmatova, 1940
translated by Jenny Wade

The "Fiery Ascent"

In 1913, at the age of 19, Vladimir Mayakovsky hit the Russian art scene like a tornado. Within a year, he published his first poems and lithographs; went on a 17-city lecture tour; published articles on Russian theater; wrote, produced and starred in his first play; and, along with his gang of friends, launched a new art movement—Futurism. Tremendously energetic and productive, he turned from one art form to another seamlessly for 20 years. He drew pictures. He exhibited paintings. He wrote, directed and acted in his own plays. He was a film star.[1] He created hundreds of agitprop posters. He wrote advertisements for cigars, cooking oil, pacifiers and sausages. He edited the avant-garde art journal *LEF*. He gave countless readings in clubs, theaters and, after the 1917 revolution, in factories, workers' clubs and Komsomol meetings. In the course of his career he collaborated with Eisenstein, Shostakovich, Meyerhold and Rodchenko.

1. In 1918, Mayakovsky wrote and starred in three silent films made at Neptun studio in St. Petersburg. The only surviving one is *The Lady and the Hooligan* (http://youtu.be/G0KF0WIrlKQ).

And he wrote poetry—love poetry, death poetry, odes to the revolution; poems dedicated to the army, to Lenin, to the Brooklyn Bridge, to the Communist Party, to skyscrapers, to the Atlantic Ocean, to the tax collector, and to his own "Beloved Self." He invites the sun over for tea, he takes Napoleon for a walk on a leash. He's a horse collapsing from exhaustion, a weepy and frightened violin, a lovesick bear floating down the river on a block of ice. He grows claws, fangs, and a tail. Elephants, giraffes, gorillas, ostriches, baby whales, camels, prostitutes, pimps, criminals and Eskimos all make appearances. He heaps insults upon the petite bourgeoisie, upon his fellow poets, and upon God Almighty ("why don't you just run along back to heaven where you belong?").

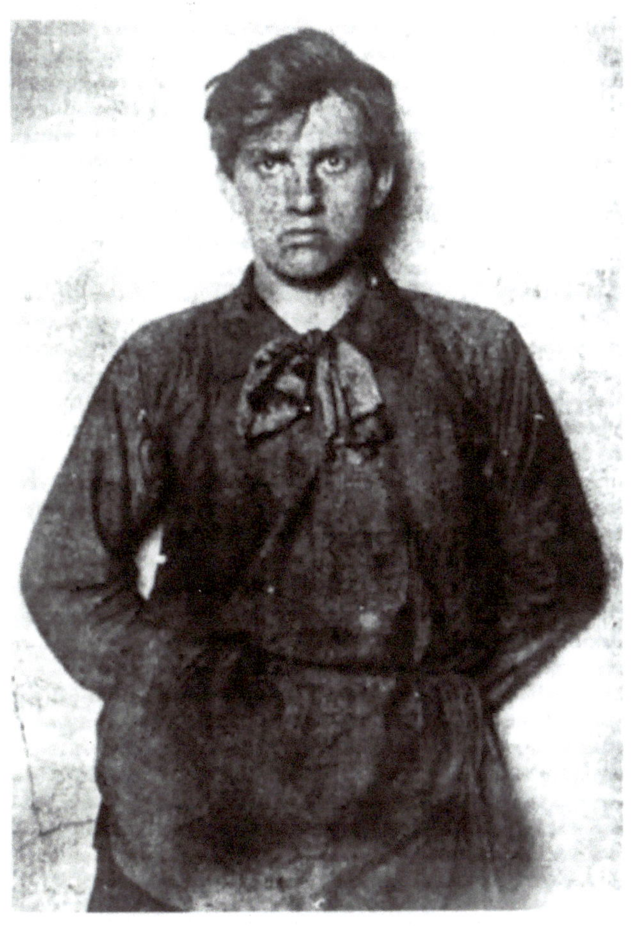

At the age of 36, at the retrospective exhibition of his life's work, he turned to a friend and asked, "Did I do enough?"

Jail

An agitator for the Bolsheviks since late adolescence, Mayakovsky was arrested at sixteen for sedition

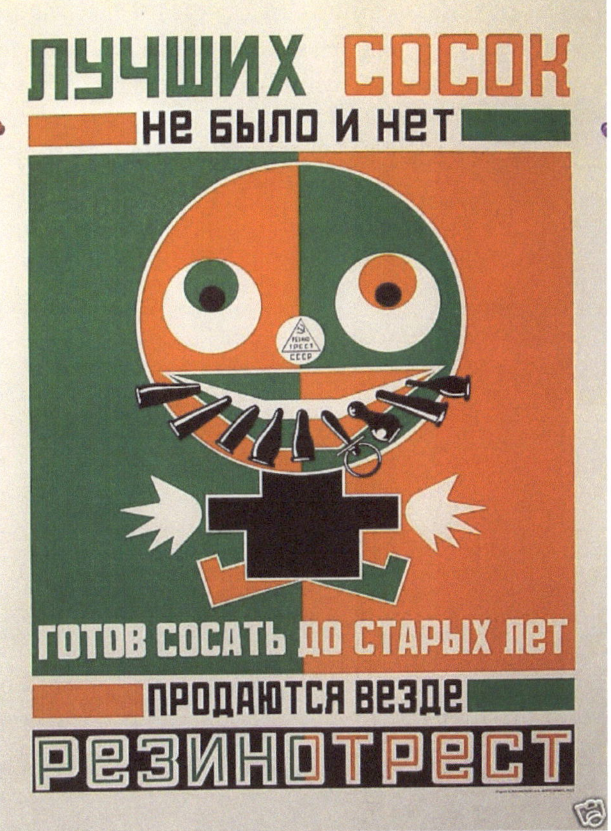

Pacifiers ad by Rodchenko and Mayakovsky, 1924. "So good, you'll want to suck on them till you're old."

in 1909 and sent to tsarist prison for the third time. Reckless, big and loud, and always willing to create a scene, before long he was placed in solitary confinement. Five months of isolation put M in an introspective frame of mind, and in reviewing his life, he realized that an art education would make him a more effective tool of the revolution. Alone in cell #103 at Butyrki prison, he immersed himself in literature and painting,[2] and made his first attempts at writing poetry. Upon his release, he gave up his activities in the political underground, let his membership in the Party lapse, and became an artist.

Art School

In 1911, after a year of working in commercial art studios, M passed the demanding entrance exam at the Moscow Institute for the Study of Painting, Sculpture and Architecture and became an art student. The Institute, against the best intentions of the

2. Courtesy of his elder sister, Ludmila, who was able to bring him books and art supplies.

administration, became an incubator for the avant-garde,[3] and M quickly fell in with the ringleaders. He found a soulmate in David Burliuk, an older student who had already produced a dozen modern art exhibits, all of them provocative, some of them scandalous.[4] Magnetic, cultured and possessing "the professional assuredness of a snake charmer,"[5] Burliuk had pulled some serious artists into his orbit—among them, the painters Kazimir Malevich, Mikhail Larionov, and Natalia Goncharova; and the poets Vasily Kamensky, Velimir Khlebnikov and Aleksey Kruchenykj—and now he added Mayakovsky to the collection.

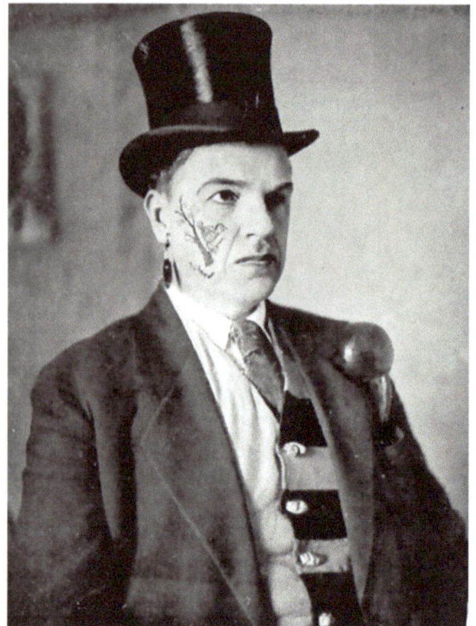

David Burliuk

Manifesto

Burliuk's coterie of artists saw themselves as agents of revolution. Sick of the realism of the previous century, sick of the mysticism of the Symbolists, sick of "byt,"[6] Burliuk and company were determined to drag art by force into the machine age.

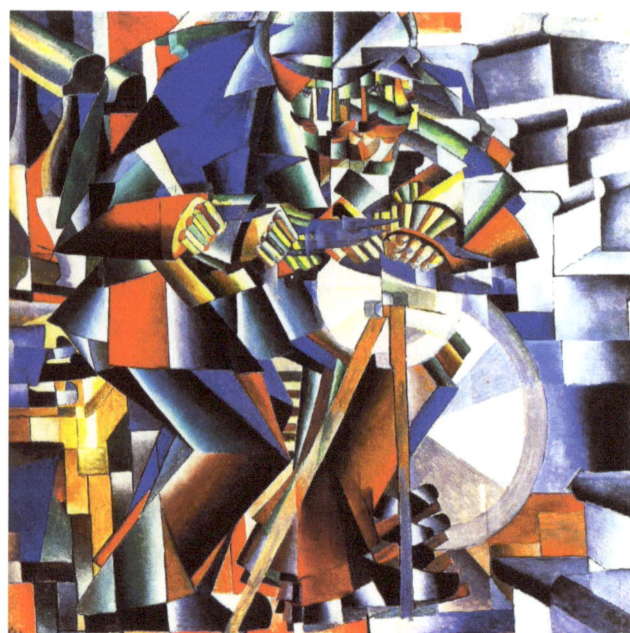

The Knife Grinder, Kazimir Malevich, 1913

Accordingly, they called themselves "The Futurists." In 1912, they issued their manifesto, *A Slap in the Face of Public Taste,* and advised their readers to "throw Pushkin, Dostoevsky, Tolstoy, etc., etc., overboard from the ship of modernity," and to "wash their hands of the filthy slime of the books written by those innumerable Leonid Andreyevs."[7] They said it was their right to "look down at their nothingness from the height of skyscrapers," to "infinitely despise all the language of the past," and to bend words, grammar, and poetic structure to suit their will. Though the poems included in the publication by M are immature and lack puissance compared to his later work (he was still only 19 years old), they are a testament to the Futurist philosophy: the poems are surreal, seemingly disjointed and nonsensical, peppered with street language, the words split into pieces and staggered across the page. There is the promise of lexical and semantic breakthroughs to come. *A Slap* was the opening volley. A flurry of Futurist pamphlets, anthologies and booklets followed. In 1913, the Futurists took their show on the road.

Tour

The first public Futurist event took place in October of 1913 at Moscow's "Hall of the Society of Art Lovers." To promote it, Burliuk had

3. Alumni included: Kazimir Malevich, Natalia Goncharova, Vladimir Tatlin, Victor Palmov, Bakulina Lyudmila, Alexander Shevchenko, Konstantin Melnikov, Yelizaveta Zvantseva and Ilya Mashkov.

4. Among the groups Burliuk did shows with: Union of Youth, Jack of Diamonds, Hylaea and Blaue Reiter in Munich. Fellow exhibitors included Chagall, Klee, Picasso and Kandinsky. At one Jack of Diamonds exhibition, painters "decorated their own naked bodies and walked as works of art through Moscow's streets." Page 212, *Natasha's Dance,* Orlando Figes.

5. Benedikt Livshits, *The one and ½ eyed Archer*, page 11.

6. The complacency and mendacity of daily life. M waged life long war against *byt*. In his last poem, composed shortly before he shot himself in the heart in 1930, he wrote: "the ship of our love is shattered on the rocky shores of the daily grind."

7. A popular, talented and prolific writer of the Silver Age.

announcements printed on toilet paper. He organized a publicity stunt: a Futurist promenade along Kuznetsky Bridge, one of Moscow's main streets, the poets marching with dogs and airplanes painted on their faces, dressed in top hats, garish ties, and

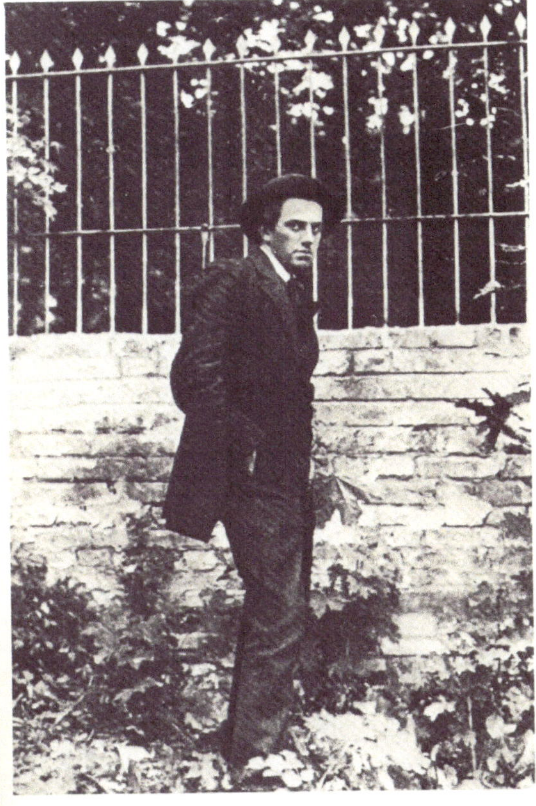

Mayakovsky in Kiev on the Futurist tour

frockcoats trimmed with rags, reciting their poetry to the crowd. Mayakovsky, wearing a bright yellow shirt with a wooden spoon as a boutonnière, was a natural performer. Standing a head taller than most everyone around him, with a stentorian voice and the demeanor of a Sicilian Mafioso, M at turns cajoled, insulted and clowned. Some were amused and curious, others confused and outraged. Fights nearly broke out, police were called in: all in all, a tremendous public relations coup.

The event sold out immediately. At the performance, Mayakovsky traded insults with the crowd, recited poetry and discussed how the ancient Egyptians produced electricity by stroking cats.[8] He explained how the world was merging into a single gigantic city, rendering nature outdated and unnecessary. Additional topics were "Folds of fat in arm-chairs," "The colorful rags of our souls," and "Orchestras of drain-pipes." While on their subsequent three-month lecture tour, M and his fellow poets would sometimes begin by sitting with each other on stage, drinking tea and casually conversing, as if the audience wasn't there. Sometimes tea would spill into the orchestra pit, sometimes onto the audience. Sometimes they would perform with a grand piano suspended over their heads. They were heckled, booed and pelted with rotten fruit and bottles. M, whom Pasternak described as "a good-looking youth of gloomy aspect with the bass voice of a deacon and the fist of a pugilist; inexhaustible, deadly, witty," overpowered every heckler. He once made the claim "I could, without even dirtying my shirtfront, nail them with my tongue to the cross of their suspenders . . . [and] roast this whole collection of insects on the

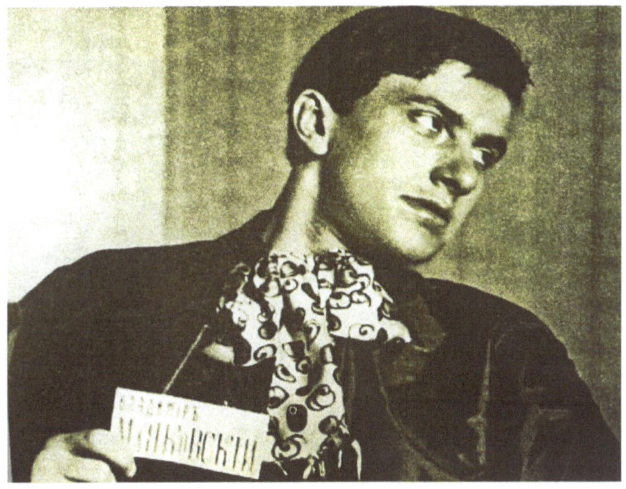

sharp turnspit of my tongue." Loud debates continued with the audience in the lobby and in the streets after shows. Theaters were surrounded by mounted police, and performances were often broken off in mid-sentence.

Pink Lantern

A FEW DAYS after the Futurist debut at Art Lovers, M and some of his gang did a poetry reading at the Pink Lantern cabaret. He unveiled his poem, "Take that!" which begins: "In an hour, one by one, your flabby fat will ooze out into the alley." And then,

8. Mayakovsky had a lifelong fascination with electricity. In his short autobiography, *I Myself*, Mayakovsky wrote that after seeing a factory lit up at night, ". . . I lost all interest in nature. Not up to date enough."

"Hey you there—you have some cabbage on your moustache, left over from your half-eaten soup," and "You there—you're so caked in makeup that you look like an oyster in a shell." Again, fighting broke out and the police came to shut down the club.

This account from the memoirs of Ivan Bunin gives a good sense of what M's performances were like. Here he describes meeting M at the opening of a Finnish art exhibition in Petrograd:

> The "flower of the Russian intelligentsia" was there to a man: famous painters, actors, writers, ministers, deputies, and one high foreign diplomat, namely the French ambassador. I sat at supper with Gorky and the Finnish painter, Axel Gallen, and Mayakovsky began his performance by suddenly coming up to us, pushing a chair between ours and helping himself from our plates and drinking out of our glasses. Gallen stared at him spellbound, just as he would probably have stared if a horse had been led into the banquet hall . . . at that moment, Milyokov, our Foreign Minister at the time, rose for an official toast and Mayakovsky dashed towards him, to the centre of the table, jumped on a chair and shouted something so obscene that Milyukov was completely flabbergasted. After a moment, regaining his control, he tried to start his speech again, "Ladies and gentlemen . . . " But Mayakovsky yelled louder than ever, and Milyukov shrugged his shoulders and sat down. Then the French ambassador rose to his feet. He was obviously convinced that the Russian hooligan would give in to him. What a hope! His voice was drowned by a deafening bellow from Mayakovksy. But this was not all. A wild and senseless pandemonium broke out. Mayakovsky supporters also began to yell, pounding their feet on the floor and their fists on the table. They screamed with laughter, whined, squeaked, snorted. But suddenly all this was quashed by a truly tragic wail of one of the Finns, a painter, who looked like a clean shaven sea-lion. Rather drunk, and pale as death, he had obviously been shaken to the core by this excess of misbehavior, and started to shout at the top of his voice, literally with tears in his eyes, one of the few Russian words he knew:
>
> *"Mnogo! Mno-go! Mno-go!"* ("too much!")[9]

And another account from one of M's closest companions during his Futurist years, Benedikt Livshits:

> At D's apartment on the Moika . . . we met several colorless young men and well-gotten-up young ladies. The latter Mayakovsky treated, I don't know by what right, like the members of his harem, though he had met them for the first time. At the table he peppered the hostess with cutting remarks, made fun of her husband, who was a quiet man and bore all of his insults without complaint...and when D., driving out of patience, dropped a remark about his filthy fingernails, he answered her with a frightful insult for which I thought we would all be asked to leave.[10]

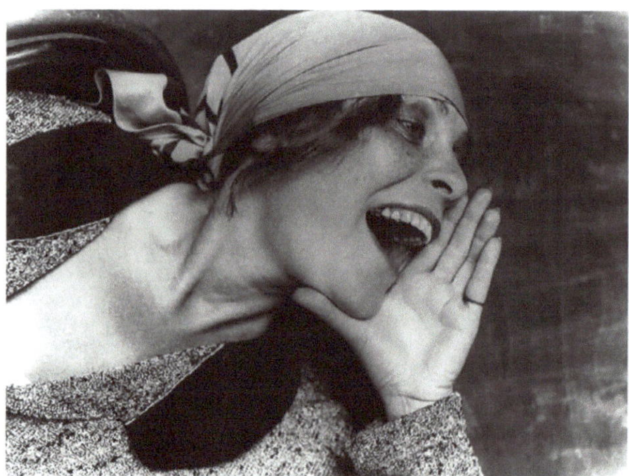

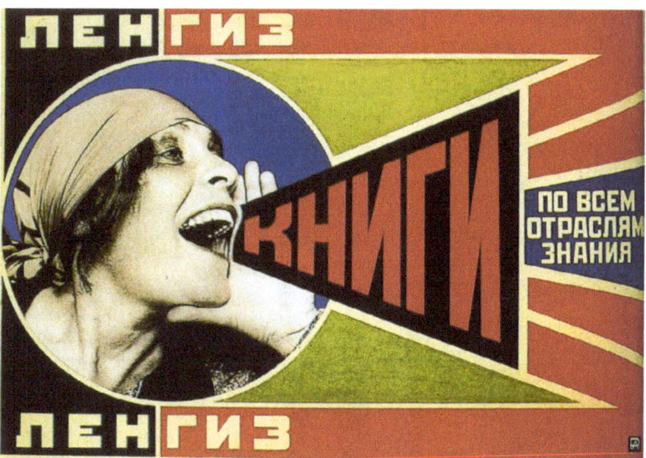

Lili Brik, photograph (left) and advertisement (right, "Books in all subjects!") both by Rodchenko.

Mayakovsky: A Tragedy

M ENDED THE whirlwind year of 1913 by writing, producing and starring in his first dramatic work,

9. *Memories and Portraits,* John Lehmann, London 1951, Ivan Bunin.

10. Livshits, *Polutoraglazyi strelets*, page 124.

Vladimir Mayakovsky: A Tragedy. Staged in St. Petersburg at the Luna Park Theater, M played the role of The Poet. All of the other characters (A Man without a Head, A Man with One Ear, A Man with One Eye and One Leg, The Man with Two Kisses, The Old Man with Old Dried-Out Black Cats, An Enormous Woman, A Woman with a Tear, A Woman with a Great Big Tear, etc.) appear as cardboard puppets, and each takes their turn either to admire or criticize the Poet. In the second act, The Poet takes center stage, adorned in a toga, crowned with a laurel wreath. He listens to each character's tale of woe, collects their tears of stone, and, Christ-like, ascends to heaven. M was, in his own words, "booed to shreds," and had to dodge the rotten fruit hurled at him. The play sold out every night.

The play is typical of of M's 1913 ouevre: brazen, absurd, egotistical to the extreme, adolescent in its intent to shock and antagonize. But it works—because of the startling images, because of his technical skill, because of the novel manner in which he expresses the harshness of city, street and machine, and because of the immediacy and vitality of his language. M captivates with his readiness, at any point, to throw himself headlong over a cliff. He holds nothing back—everything is exposed and open to ridicule. Underneath this lies an impressive core of courage, self-conviction and inner strength—a wholehearted, almost unthinking determination to stand his ground against any onslaught.

The Poems

The first poem is read by Mayakovsky himself, the latter two by his longtime lover Lili Brik, who inspired his greatest love poems ("Backbone Flute," "About That," Lilichka! Instead of a Letter," etc.). She also served as a muse for Rodchenko, who used her as a model for book covers and advertisements. Along with her husband, Osip Brik, Lili was a major aid in managing, editing, and publishing M's work.

In my translations, I have made no attempt to match the Russian rhyme or meter. Instead I tried to bring out the tone and meaning while staying as literal as possible. The background information above should help put the poems into context.

А вы могли бы?

Я сразу смазал карту будня,
плеснувши краску из стакана;
я показал на блюде студня
косые скулы океана.
На чешуе жестяной рыбы
прочел я зовы новых губ.
А вы
ноктюрн сыграть
могли бы
на флейте водосточных труб?

And could you?

Right now I smeared the map of Monday through Friday,
splashing paint out of a glass;
on a plate of gravy
I showed you the slanted cheekbones of the ocean.
On the scales of a store-front tin fish
I read the proclamations of new lips.
And you
do you think you could play a nocturne
on a flute
made out of drainage pipes?

From the Futurist collection, *The Missal of the Three,* published in 1913. Illustrated by Vladimir Tatlin.

LISTEN TO THESE POEMS, READ BY MAYAKOVSKY AND LILI BRIK, HERE:
www.sensitiveskinmagazine.com/mayakovsky

КОФТА ФАТА

Я сошью себе черные штаны
из бархата голоса моего.
Желтую кофту из трех аршин заката.
По Невскому мира, по лощеным полосам его,
профланирую шагом Дон-Жуана и фата.

Пусть земля кричит, в покое обабившись:
"Ты зеленые весны идешь насиловать!"
Я брошу солнцу, нагло осклабившись:
"На глади асфальта мне хорошо грассировать!"

Не потому ли, что небо голубо,
а земля мне любовница в этой праздничной чистке,
я дарю вам стихи, веселые, как би-ба-бо,
и острые и нужные, как зубочистки!

Женшины, любящие мое мясо, и эта
девушка, смотрящая на меня, как на брата,
закидайте улыбками меня, поэта,-
я цветами нашью их мне на кофту фата!

The Dandy's Jacket

I'll sew myself a pair of black trousers
from the velvet of my own voice.
A yellow jacket from three yards of sunset.
I'll saunter along the boulevards of the world,
along its burnished stripes,
like Don Juan—dressed to kill.

Let the earth yell and scream, overripe from too much rest:
"Spring is fresh and green, and you're going out to violate her!"
I throw myself at the sun, smirking,
"Too bad—it feels good to glide along the asphalt."

Isn't it because the sky is blue
And the earth is my lover, all cleaned up for the occasion,
I give you poetry. It's fun, like puppets,
and sharp and useful, like toothpicks.

Women love me, and now this
girl, looking at me as intimately as a sister.
Toss your smiles to me, the poet.
I'll sew them onto my fancy jacket like flowers.

Written in 1913, published in 1914 in *Number 1 – 2 of the First Journal of the Russian Futurists.*

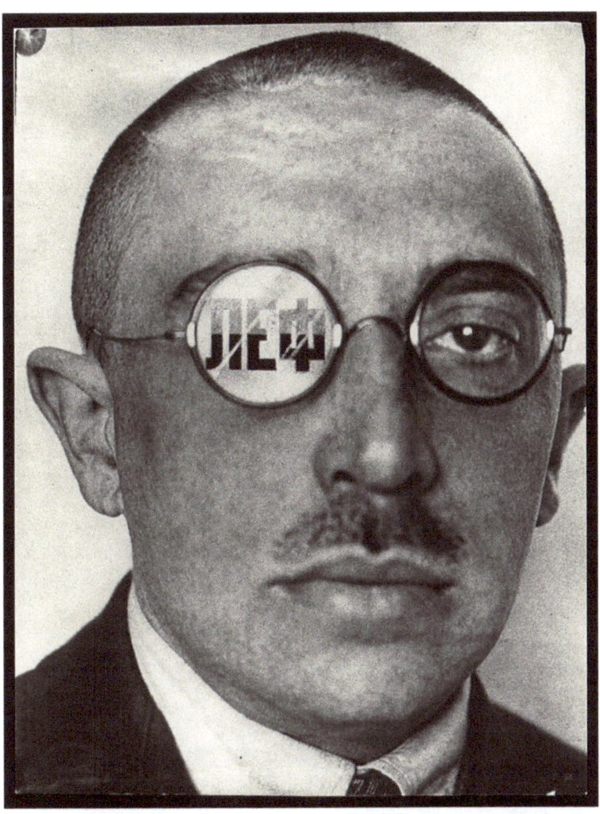

Osip Brik, photograph by Rodchenko, cover of *LEF*

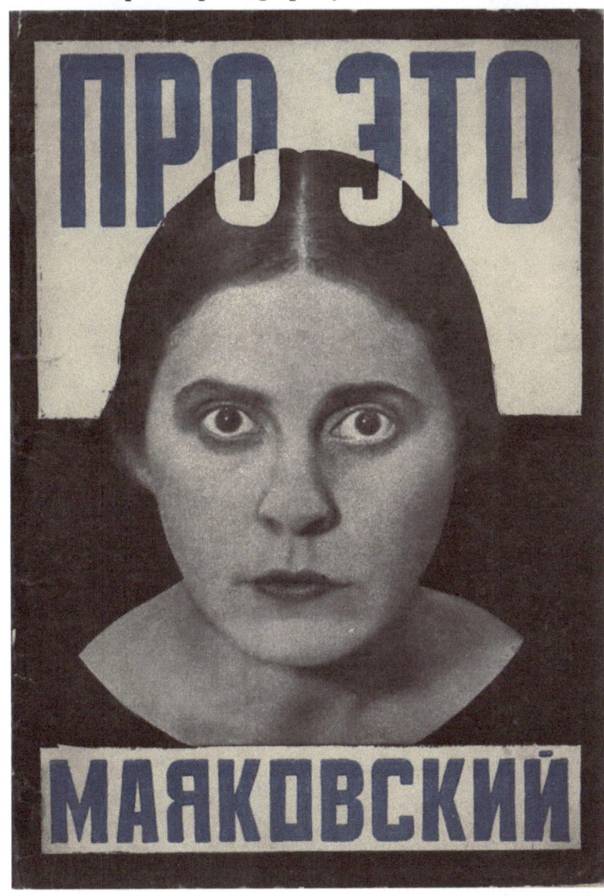

Alexander Rodchenko, cover of the book, *About That*, by Vladimir Mayakovsky, 1923

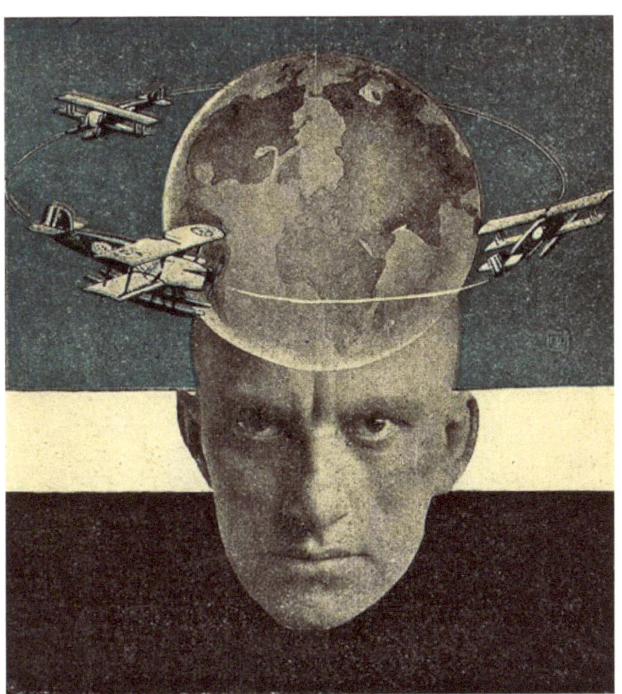

Rodchenko, Photomontage for rear cover of Mayakovsky's *A Conversation with a Tax-Collector about Poetry*, 1926

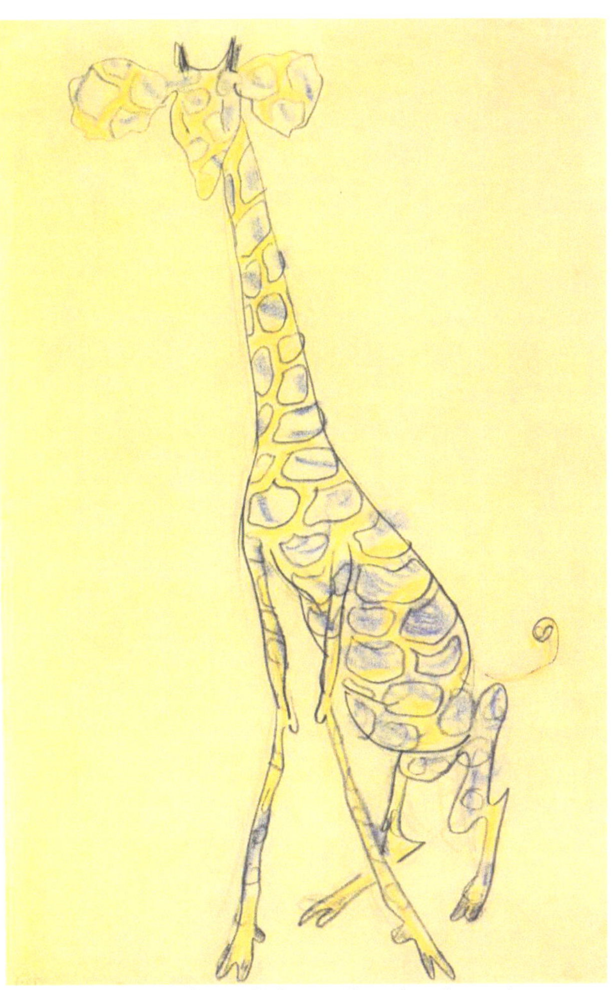

V. Mayakovsky, "A giraffe," 1913. Pastel and pencil on paper.

Из улицы в улицу

у-
лица.
Лица
у
догов
годов рез-
че. Че-
рез
железных коней
с окон бегущих домов
прыгнули первые кубы.
Лебеди шей колокольных,
гнитесь в силках проводов!
В небе жирафий рисунок готов
выпестрить ржавые чубы.
Пестр, как форель,
сын
безузорной пашни.
Фокусник
рельсы
тянет из пасти трамвая,
скрыт циферблатами башни.
Мы завоеваны!
Ванны.
Души.
Лифт.
Лиф души расстегнули.
Тело жгут руки.
Кричи, не кричи:
«Я не хотела!» —
резок
жгут
муки.
Ветер колючий
трубе
вырывает
дымчатой шерсти клок.
Лысый фонарь
сладострастно снимает
с улицы
черный чулок.

From street to street

The
street.
Faces
of
mastiffs
are sharper
than years.
The buildings are running,
and the first cubes are leaping
from the windows
through the iron horses.
Swans of bell necks
bend into nooses of electric wire!
In the sky a cartoon giraffe is about to show off
the speckled highlights of his rusty forelocks.
Dappled like a trout,
the son
of common fields.
A street magician,
hidden behind the clocktower faces,
is pulling rails
out of the streetcar's mouth.
We've been overrun!
Bathtubs.
Showers.
An elevator.
The bodice of your soul is undone.
Hands burn your body.
Go ahead and scream:
"I didn't want to!"
The rope
cuts
and burns.
The thorny wind
tears
wooly clumps of smoke
from the chimney.
A bald-headed lamppost
lasciviously pulls off
the street's
black stocking.

Published in *A Trap For Judges, Number 2,* 1913. The painter V. Malevich described this poem, with its vivid shifting images, as "versified cubism." Many of the phrases can be read backwards or forwards. M said the poem was inspired by a streetcar ride along the Sadovo-Sukharvskaya. The clocktower would be Sukharev tower, which was torn down in the 1930s.

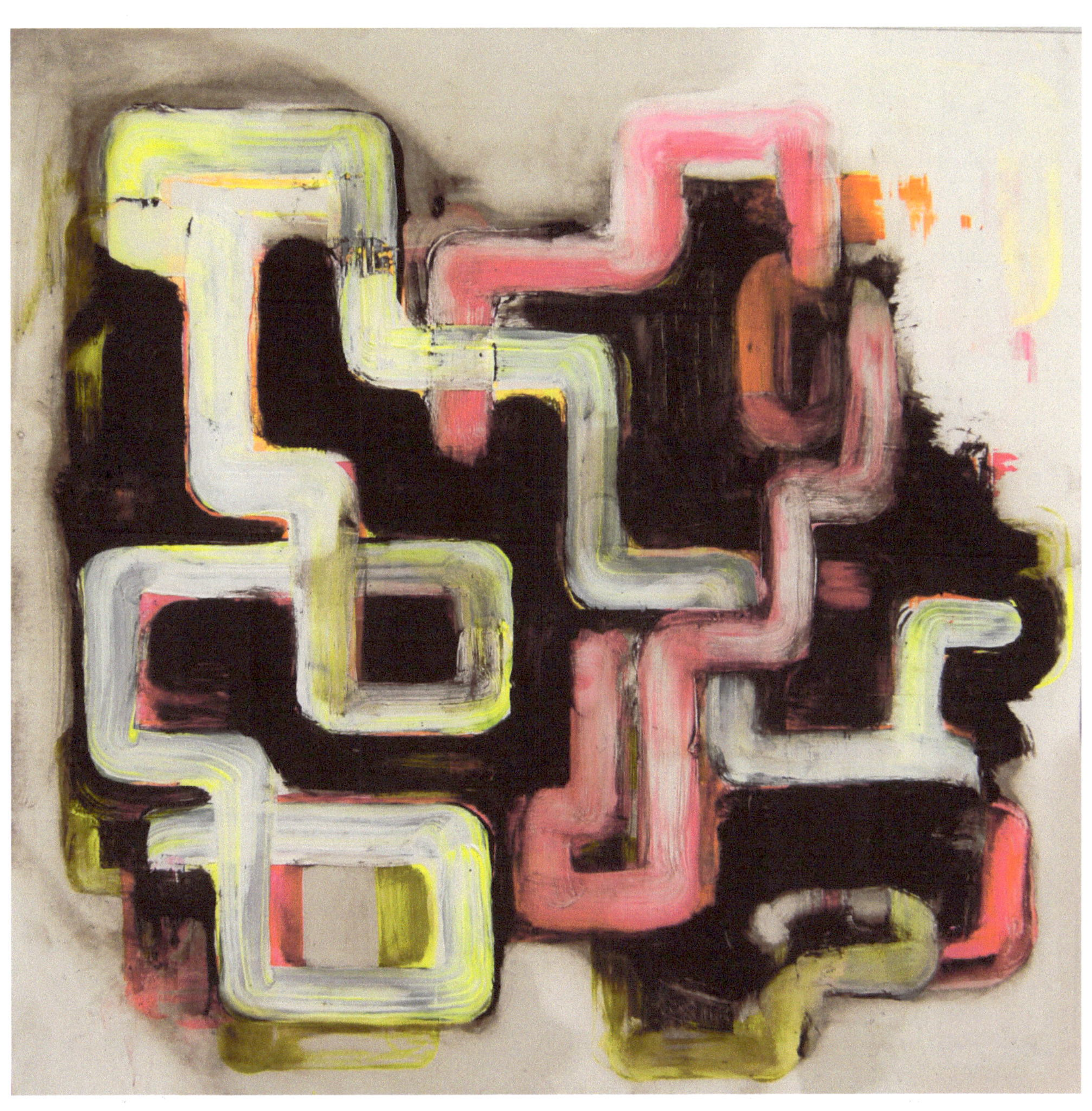

Claritas, oil and acrylic on panel, Justine Frischmann, 2012,

Killing Williamsburg

Bradley Spinelli

RUMORS

It started like a whisper, a fall breeze through the drying leaves of September's trees. We overheard words dropped like cigarette butts and unwanted taxi receipts, snippets of clandestine conversation intercepted while standing in line at the deli or crowding onto the morning L train.

I began to wonder if people in the neighborhood were doing more drugs than usual, because, at first, the buzz of the streets took on a feeling of excitement. People seemed more on their toes. The once-removed attitude I had come to expect seemed to quicken a little. I thought everyone was suddenly looking to score. Or that perhaps the slight drop in temperature or change in barometric pressure had brought about a reverse vernal effect, and everyone was looking to go home with somebody new.

Veracruz on Bedford was full as always. I never went there. I wasn't cool or tattooed enough to join the mobbing slew of hipsters lining up to slurp frozen 'ritas at happy hour, arrogantly peering out the open French doors. But now, as I walked by, the eyes spooled out to me, begging me to tell them something, anything, that would satiate their curiosity, however briefly, and give them something to whisper in the dead hour before bedtime.

There were more sirens than usual, whining off into the distance at all hours, singing their sad song of delight, bouncing off the walls of buildings and down sidewalks that scrolled out of sight, blaring by in a swirl of lights that splattered our wonderstruck faces with crimson and blue. Something strange and mildly sinister was clearly afoot, but there was no answer forthcoming, and we tried to tune out or turn down the din and incorporate it into our lives as background music, like chittering cicadas and staccato sprinklers oscillating back and forth over the green lawns of a long Indian summer in suburbia.

The papers gave us no clue. We checked the metro section and found nothing out of the ordinary, and the obits were no help either. But we knew. Somehow we all knew. Something was happening. Our world was changing around us, and it was bigger than the influx of yuppies and trustifarians, bigger than the impending grand opening of the mini-mall in the old Real Form Girdle factory, bigger than Plan Eat Thai moving to a new space. There was a shadow falling over us, an uncertainty. We could feel that uncertainty in our bones and our boots, in our carrot juice and our bagels, in our 3:55 final shot and our 4:00-in-the-morning slice, in the *Village Voice* ink on our fingers, in our American Spirits.

Anecdotes were traded by osmosis. Sitting at a bar or coffee shop, we could smell each other's thoughts, and each unfinished story became urban legend overnight. This is the way we learn in the city, through innuendo and rumor.

An ambulance arrives at a residence and there's a woman shrieking on the street. Passersby see the gurney, the shrouded figure, but no one knows what happened, or why. "He was only 35, maybe younger." "The girl went back home, out West somewhere."

Half-swallowed anecdotes and rumors became fact, stepping the transubstantiating boundary between the ephemeral and the realm of the solid, the undeniable.

Olive and I, no different from any other couple in the 'hood, bent over the kitchen table night after night as the light faded, the sun setting earlier and earlier.

"Supposedly she took pills."

"I hear he stabbed himself somehow. A kitchen knife or something."

"Gas. The oven, I think."

"A light socket? I don't buy it. There's not enough juice in these old buildings to kill."

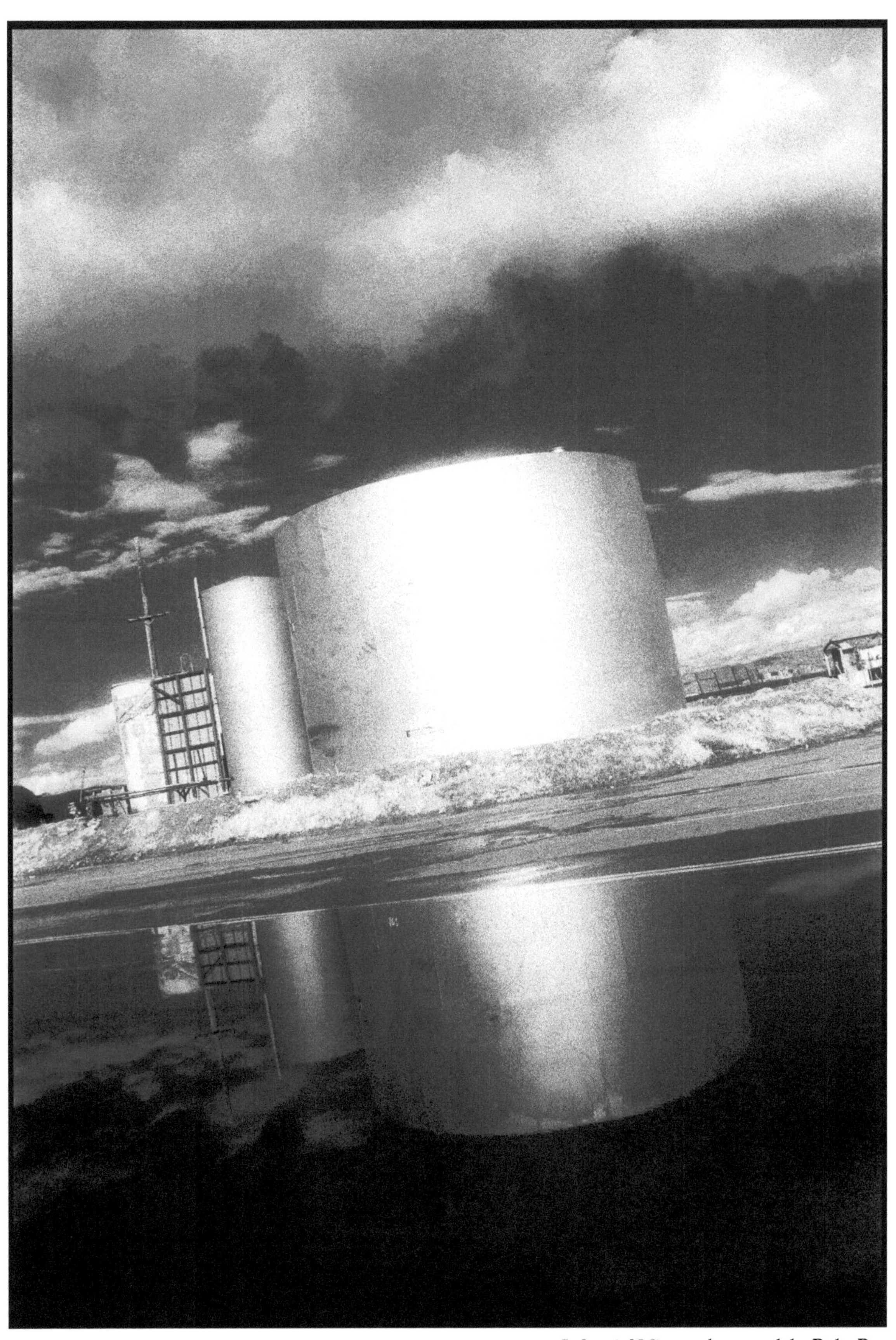

Industrial Mirage, photograph by Ruby Ray

"It sounded crazy, but you should have seen the look on her face."

It wasn't anyone we knew. Not yet, anyway.

BOMB-OUT

Crews had started to pop up in Manhattan and, just as in Williamsburg, it seemed that a gang-style grassroots approach netted more survivors than a centrally organized effort. You can only trust the people you run with, the kids who will save your ass because you saved theirs yesterday, whether that means fighting off a maniac in the throes of a suicide attempt gone bad, swatting away rabid rats, or just offering an encouraging comment to someone about to slip into despair.

"All right, I'm going in," Jack said. He gave me a nod and I threw the door open. We were investigating a short, squatty building off of Bushwick that was rumored to be a mess. Other crews had backed away from it, and I was determined to clean it up. We were on the top floor—you always work your way down—and this was the first apartment we'd tried to get into.

We all started yelling as Jack opened the door again and the eight of us darted into the apartment with our eyes stinging. Rats swarmed about our feet, disoriented and scrambling for cover. I stepped on one and almost fell.

The door blew open again and Jack jumped back into the hallway. I slammed the door behind him.

"Rats! Holy shit, I've never seen so many rats," he said.

"All right, let's fucking bomb it." I made the gesture for "bombs" to one of the huge Poles, who was carrying most of our auxiliary effects, shaking my hand like a spray can and making a *psssst* sound. The Pole handed me a four-pack of bug bombs, the kind you use to clear a house of fleas or cockroaches. They don't kill the rats, but the rats hate them and will generally leave the room when they smell the foul gas.

Luz tied her handkerchief around her face, and her voice came out muffled. "How many years are we taking off our lives with this stuff?"

"I don't know, babe," I answered. "How many have you got?" I put my handkerchief on like an Old West cowboy in a dust storm.

Chico, Luz and I shook bombs and Jack pulled the door open and we hit the buttons on the bombs and threw them in. Jack slammed the door and silently counted to twenty to give the rats a chance to get out. We all started yelling as Jack opened the door again and the eight of us darted into the apartment with our eyes stinging. Rats swarmed about our feet, disoriented and scrambling for cover. I stepped on one and almost fell. I caught myself and heard the cute girl from Group D squealing and Chico muttering under his breath.

"Don't even look! Fucking fan out, people! Let's get out of here!"

The Poles disappeared into a bedroom, reappeared through the haze carrying a corpse, and started for the door.

"Window! Window!" I shouted, and picked up a TV remote from a side table and threw it at the window to get their attention. You don't have time in a bomb-out to mess with stairs. The Poles broke the window out with a boot and a gloved fist and tossed the body. They headed back into the same room and I knew there were more.

"Phil, follow!"

Phil and the cute girl from Group D followed them in. There was another doorway, and Luz and Chico came out pulling a bloated corpse. There was a corpse on the front couch, and Jack and I hoisted it up and out the window. As we were about to dump it over, a rat fell from the curtains and Jack jumped.

"Chingale!"

Luz buzzed past me, stepping over swarming rats. "That room's clean."

"The back," I said, pointing in the direction of the Poles. We took a step in unison and saw the Poles coming out with another, and behind them, Phil and the cute girl from Group D, each of them cradling a small, crumpled shape. They had found the remains of two dead children, no older than eight or nine. Tears streamed down the cute girl's face, and I didn't think it was just because of the gas.

I took the body from her hands and barked at Chico, "Get her out of here!" and tossed the body out the window, watching it fall four floors to the grassy front yard. Phil followed suit and gave me the sign for "clean," like a salute that missed.

"Go! Go! Go!" I screamed, and we all piled out of the apartment stumbling over each other and the running rats, and Jack slammed the door. A rat squirmed under and Chico shot it dead out of spite.

We ran downstairs and fell outside, collapsing on the front stoop and panting for breath and tearing at our masks and scratching at our tearing eyes. Phil passed out water and we tried to recover. As soon as I could breathe, I reached for my cell phone.

"Neil? It's me. Listen, we gotta get some more guys over here. Yeah. I'm at Bushwick and Devoe. It's fucking bad. If anyone calls in, get them over here. And tell Bernie to send someone over with more bombs. Yeah, it's that bad. Right on."

I hung up and shut my eyes, tight, watching the blood flow through my lids and trying to make the headache go away. I opened them quickly when I heard someone screaming.

The cute girl from Group D was plunging her knife into her breast. Luz was wrapped around her, trying to wrest the knife out of her hand.

"Get away from her!" I barked. "It's too late!"

The cute girl managed a swipe at Luz and cut her a good one across the forearm. Chico grabbed Luz and pulled her away. She was yelling obscenities and thrashing her head from side to side as the cute girl from Group D shoved the knife in and out of her own chest until her torso was a bloody confetti of shredded sternum and tissue. She lay flat on her back in the matted grass with the knife protruding, her hands out to either side of her cocked head, hands open and begging for forgiveness.

"Damn it, damn it, damn it, goddamn it," Luz spat as Chico tried getting her to sit down on the stoop so he could look at her bleeding wound. One of the Poles took a blanket out of a rucksack and laid it across the girl's cute, dead face so we wouldn't have to look at it. I reached for the cell phone and called Bernie.

"It's me. Yeah, Bernie, I'm sure you're busy. You need to get someone over here, right now. Bushwick and Devoe. I don't care. Leave them there. I DON'T FUCKING CARE, BERNIE, I GOT A MAN DOWN AND I WANT HER REMAINS REMOVED." I hung up, sat down on the curb and ran my hands across my stubbly head.

I've seen better days.

I must have seen better days.

LONGING

I MISS THE yuppies.

I miss the Williamsburg bohemian yuppies with their designer dogs and their square-shouldered swagger, the women's hot black slit skirts and minimalist makeup, the men's casual slouch jeans and no-starch shirts. I miss the Upper East Side mavens with their haughty Oscar de la Renta noses, their Lexus smiles and gleaming BMW teeth. I miss the West Village old-schoolers with their pretentious and patient endurance of the come-hither gay boys, the "What has the neighborhood come to?" and the "I have to leave town on Gay Pride and Halloween," and I miss the homosexual yuppie ecstasy culture, wannabe Republican and insisting "We're here, we're queer, get used to it." I miss the Technicolor yuppies clogging the former drug jungles of Alphabet City, slinking down lettered avenues all dressed in black and anointed with delicate scents of microbrew beers and Nat Sherman cigarettes, gathering in hibiscus clusters to preen and guffaw over the latest office gossip and last week's episode of *Sex and the City*. I miss the Union Square late-afternoon sunset watch on the south-side steps, the huddled backpack-bearing masses yearning to spend free, to worship at the altar of the Virgin Megastore and pray for more meaningful one-night stands and more Helmut Lang minimalism in their lives. I miss the afternoon Soho runway of crowded, narrow streets speckled with oversize sunglasses and begging-to-be-recognized wish-I-were-a-model nymphettes, tiny and anorexic in Calista Flockhart glee, seemingly on the edge of slipping down a storm drain and disappearing in a dreamlike flush of glamour, laced with the delicate aroma of Obsession by Calvin Klein. I miss the Central Park matching jogging outfits and the Rollerbladers decked out in fashion-forward crash gear, the hushed conversations held between panting breaths, betwixt the rhythm of $200 running shoes with patented features—a peacock mating ritual in pitch-black shades and Lycra action wear barely containing the whimsical yearnings of the flesh. I miss the Tribeca cavalcade of overpriced restaurants owned by celebrities, the reservation-required dominance of overbearing, prettier-than-you hostesses and swishy waiters who specialized in drinks or order-taking only, leaving the food-running and bussing to the hordes of minority minimum-wagers and welcoming with open arms anyone with the scratch to order delicacies unerringly, drink from the correct glass, shovel with the proper fork, tip exorbitantly and never break the façade of a stiff smile and cheery, shallow conversation—the agreed-upon convention that dining in public is a private affair. I miss Coffee Shop on Union Square, Layla on West Broadway, Spa on 13th—all the magnets for yuppies

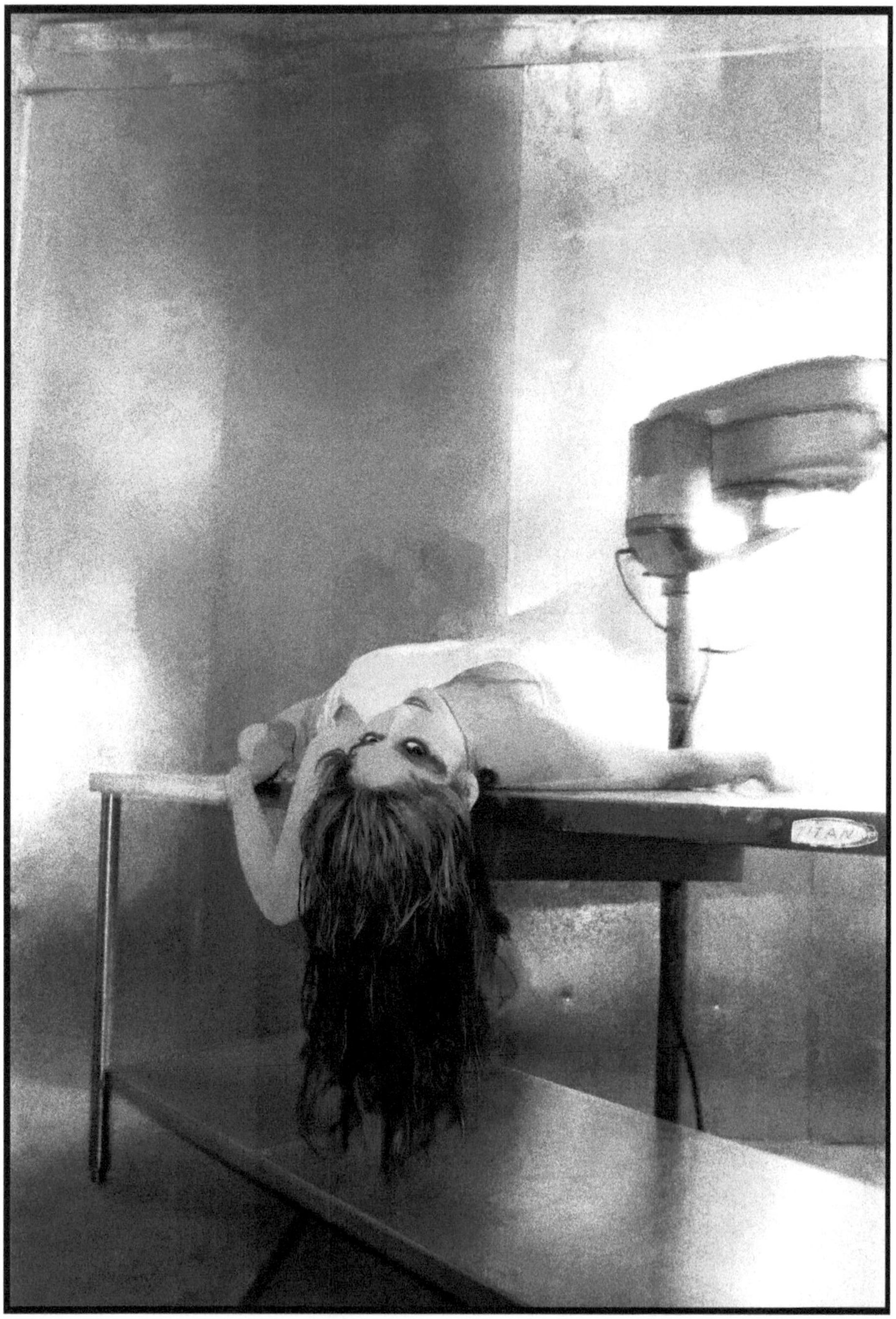

Odalisque on Cold Metal, photograph by Ruby Ray

and their money-grubbing ilk, those simple-minded capitalists with their vacuous simplicity, drawn to the simple pleasures of fine clothes; high-paying, low-impact desk labor; and tasty, sweet cocktails that bring lithe intoxication, weak-kneed recovery, and for-a-limited-time-only sexual pleasure exercised in reckless abandon in a stranger's apartment, hushing cries and weeps of orgasm under bedclothes and fancy feather pillows, buried below the radar of a roommate's ear.

I miss the YUPs, the SYPs, the GYPs; the slackers, the hipsters, the whiners; the come-latelies, the girl Fridays, the go-to guys; the suits, the stiffs, the execs; the moguls, the magnates, the self-appointed magistrates; the CEOs, the CPOs, the COOs; the indifferent and ungainly and impressive. I miss them in their terrifying and alienating hauteur, snobbery, selfishness, hedonism, aggression, ambition, delusion, subordination, didacticism, autonomy, and superiority. I miss their takeovers; their sitcoms; their gather-round-the-water-cooler gossip; their rampant greed; their blind subservience to a status quo of their own design; their unerring fallibility in any social situation requiring tact; their pushy manner on the sidewalks and subways; their malicious, derisive glares at street people, the homeless, and blue-collar losers alike; the *Wall Street Journals* tucked in the armpits of their thousand-dollar suits; the Gucci handbags slung viciously alongside their graceless, full-figured or slender-hipped bodies; their phony laughs and guffaws; their practiced smiles wielded mercilessly on the "service industry"—their "Keep the change" and their "Ciao."

I miss their bad example and my bitter reaction and contorted oaths. I miss the color they add to the sidewalks, the density and elbowing they add to a barroom. I miss the hated wheels of progress and consumerism that they continue turning, tirelessly.

I miss their differences from and their similarities to me. I miss their bad example and my bitter reaction and contorted oaths. I miss the color they add to the sidewalks, the density and elbowing they add to a barroom. I miss the hated wheels of progress and consumerism that they continue turning, tirelessly. I miss their humanity, epitomizing weakness and strength in every crushed white cigarette, every raised taxi-hailing hand, every signed deal and every Starbucks double mocha latte Frappuccino and every secluded online call to Cosmo.com to deliver the latest Gwyneth Paltrow movie, a bag of Pepperidge Farm Milanos, a tub of Häagen-Dazs and a bottle of Pellegrino.

I miss them, more than anything, not for the hole of hatred I once harbored in my heart for them, but for their livid, animate existence purely, no matter how paltry or pale or simpering they ever appeared to me. I miss them because they were alive. They walked, they talked, they ordered a slice. They took cabs and they rode the subway, they made money and spent it, they were upright and mobile. They breathed, they ate, they shit; their hearts beat and their eyes wept. They sweated. They came. They wiped the crust from their eyes in the morning and the jam from their toes at night. They showered and brushed their teeth. They worried. They loved. They hated with abandon. They felt small and inadequate; powerful and fulfilled; empty and frustrated; abandoned and blamed; championed and adored.

They lived.

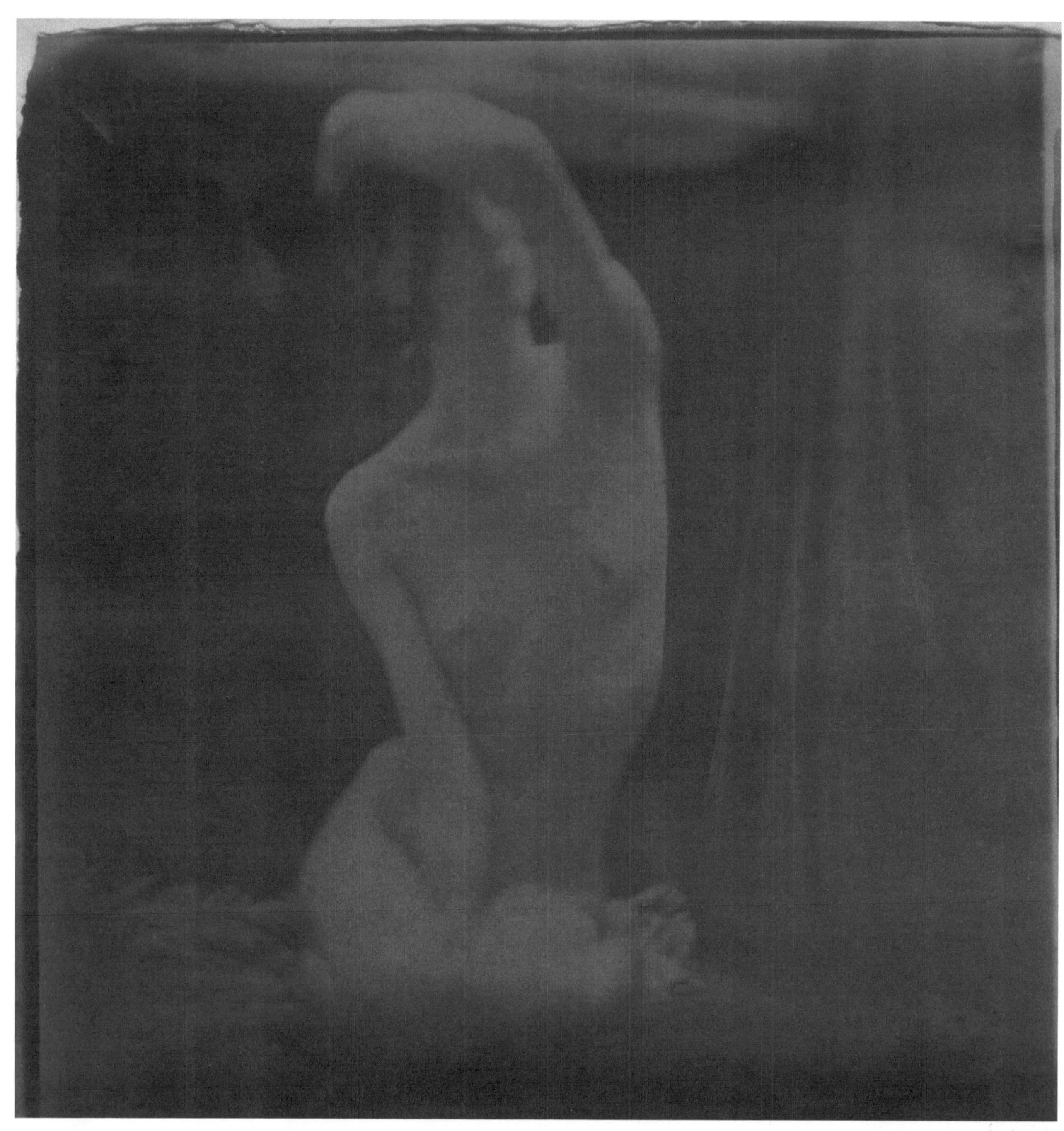

photograph by Hal Hirshorn

Bump Your Ass Off

Anna Mockler

We was going to be late if he didn't hurry up, he was cutting it really close, and I was almost mad with Rudy if he was going to make us late for the end of the world at Coney. I looked at my Roylex and I said patient, it never does no good to get quick with Rudy, I said, "Old buddy you should wear the shirt I give you to wear," because he don't see right, Rudy, his eyes roll up like and wander, he sees blue, he says banana, he's cross-wired since this dermatology intern pulled his brain out of our mom with forceps, so Rudy he can take a long time, see, choosing what to wear.

This is why I don't usually make a fuss, but it was the end of the world, see, and it was going to be at Coney, right, and we had to be there on the dot and looking sharp. That's what I figured. If we wanted to get good seats and all. We was going to remember this for the rest of our lives, right, so I wanted us both to be looking fine and right on time. Because you don't get a second chance to make a first impression.

So I pull the green shirt with the crocodile over Rudy's head and I show him how the belt closes and he puts on his own shoes which goes pretty quick now I got him the Velcro-close kind and I hang his key around his neck inside his shirt and we walk out the door only ten minutes late. As we go down the stairs, I tell the tale, how he don't talk to anybody he don't see me shake their hand first, he stay right with me even if there's a dog on the train he hold onto me, he don't pick up anything at all off the street, and etcetera like that.

We walk the twelve blocks to Union Square even though was I by myself I'd take the L and transfer but Rudy he gets confused walking underground, he starts talking loud how he can't see the sky and how come's that, so we walk to the Q train which is fast to Coney and we need to get there fast. I keep my arm around his shoulder and he walks just as fast as me, he's playing fish, his lips push in and out and that's fine so long as his legs keep going like a person, I tell him he's doing real good and he goes to stop and tell me all about it, but I say, "Tell me on the train," and he keeps walking. He's being so good. I'm real proud of him.

Getting him through the turnstile is always tricky, this is why we don't use those entrances that have like revolving cages, if I pulled him out of one of those once I done it a hundred times, no it's got to be regular turnstiles and that's what they have at 14th and Fourth and that's what we go through, I swipe the Metrocard and tell him, "Go!" and he goes right through, it's lucky, there's a little white dog sticking out of this lady's bag and Rudy goes right through after the dog but, still lucky, even though I have to swipe three times before it reads my card I catch up to him before he can pet the dog or pet the lady which either one takes up a lot of time which time we don't have. We have to get to Coney if we want good seats. Rudy nods when I say this and walks away from the dog which is going uptown and we walk fast down the stairs and a Q pulls in and there's two seats facing backwards, lucky a third time, so Rudy and me sit down and spread out our legs and I show him the sports pages until we come out on the elevated tracks and then he shows me the trees and the birds and names the different kinds of litter. "Plastic bottle. Glass bottle. Coke can." He likes to say "Coke can" so much that sometimes I don't tell him the right name because he gets a smile on his face saying, "Coke can, Coke can," and meanwhile I can check how the Yankees are doing which I'm not supposed to do because we're a Mets family, always been a Mets family, and I'm behind them 200 percent, I mean everybody gets slumps, but if it's going to be the end of the world I figure I'll sneak a look at how the Bombers are doing. I shake my head. "Glass southpaw," I tell Rudy. "Glass pawpaw?" he says. "Never mind, it's okay," I tell him, and we go on all the way to Coney like that, me shaking my head and him saying, "New paper. Plastic bag. New paper. Coke can, Coke can." He don't say it too loud or nothing and nobody's paying attention anyhow, they're putting on their makeup or talking in their cell phones, getting ready for the end of the world at Coney, little kids is running around they parents paying them no mind and this one couple is going at it hot and heavy which made me think about Marcella who I'm not going to see before the end of the world, I figure, since she kept wanting us to go out just me and her without Rudy who she said was creepy so I told her goodbye, she was hot, Marcella, but there's going to be a lot of spilled milk at the end of the world so what's the use of crying about a few drops of it? I show Rudy this big bird out the other side of the train so he don't get all upset by this couple making out. "Vulture," he says.

Finally, finally, we get to Coney and I put my arm around Rudy's shoulder and we walk to the shooting pond where we're all supposed to meet, he stays right with me in the crowd and I tell him what a good job he's doing and he smiles which always cheers me up and all the way there, lucky again, nobody says nothing about how we mixing the races or we weirdos holding hands or nothing, we stop in front of the bumper cars and me and Rudy say, right along with this woman who comes out of the loudspeakers, we say, "Bump! Bump your ass off!" and the little kids which we used to be, plus grown-ups too, zoom around under the disco music bumping each other all they can. "Bump, bump yo rassoff," Rudy says, and I say, "That's right," and we walk as fast as we can which isn't very fast because everybody and his wife, I swear on my mother's grave, has come to Coney for the end of the world.

Still, we make good time and in fact we're early at the meet spot, the place where you shoot at the animals by the pond, the bear and the raccoon and the tin cup. One time I hit the bear and made him stand all up so now every time we go there Rudy's all like, "Make the bear jump! Make the bear jump!" but no time for that now, we got to meet our people and get good seats and that's what we got to do. That's what I tell him. "Okay," says Rudy.

How lucky is this? All our people are on time, Cassandra, Donnell, Ramona and Vernon and all, they're on time. Isn't that something? I shake all their hands so Rudy knows it's okay and we all hug each other and Donnell says Bernice grown another inch since I saw her last month and Cassandra got her hair all up and then coming down braids and Vernon got a new job they give him his own separate cell phone, he's that important, and we talk like that for a while and then I look at my Roylex and I say, "Okay, let's get this show on the road."

This is why I don't usually make a fuss, but it was the end of the world, see, and it was going to be at Coney, right, and we had to be there on the dot and looking sharp.

We get our seats and I buy Rudy a ice cream at highway-robbery prices from a guy with a cooler, which if I was in charge guys wouldn't holler "Ice cream!" in public places where they put ideas into people's heads. I wouldn't let them. We sit there for half an hour and Donnell says he can't believe they're holding the curtain for the end of the world, and Ramona says ain't that just typical, they waiting for more crowd, and Cassandra says they probably nervous doing a one-shot stand like this, and Vernon says that's right, he says it's not like they going to get a chance to polish they performance, and all of them laughing but I don't laugh because sure enough Rudy spilled some ice cream on his seat and I have to wipe it up before he gets down and starts licking that chair, who knows where that chair been, but they all laughing right along.

At last the curtain goes up and this big fat guy on the stage shouts we're going to see "Got a damn run!" and we all shout back "Got a damn run!" which our mom used to say is only what you can expect with dime-store nylons, she said you get what you pay for.

The whole rest of it I couldn't figure out what kind of language they was talking, all holding onto these big sticks and shouting at them, and neither could Donnell or Vernon or Cassandra. Ramona says they was speaking Yiddish which I ask how would she know? She says it was on account of she works in the garment district. "They got their own whole language?" says Cassandra, and Donnell and Vernon and me say, all at the same time, "Hush up," and Rudy almost falls off his chair laughing.

The people on the stage they shout at their sticks and carry women around and set one of them on fire except not really and then the other women comb their long hair down around their knees, then there's more of they hit each other with sticks and stick each other with blades and fall down dead except they wasn't really dead they was just getting ready to shout some more—I maybe would have understood it more better if Rudy didn't keep showing me these vultures that was flying around the old parachute jump, him and me took turns looking through binoculars at these birds flying and flying. It was more interesting than all these people shouting at their sticks, for sure, plus it kept him quiet.

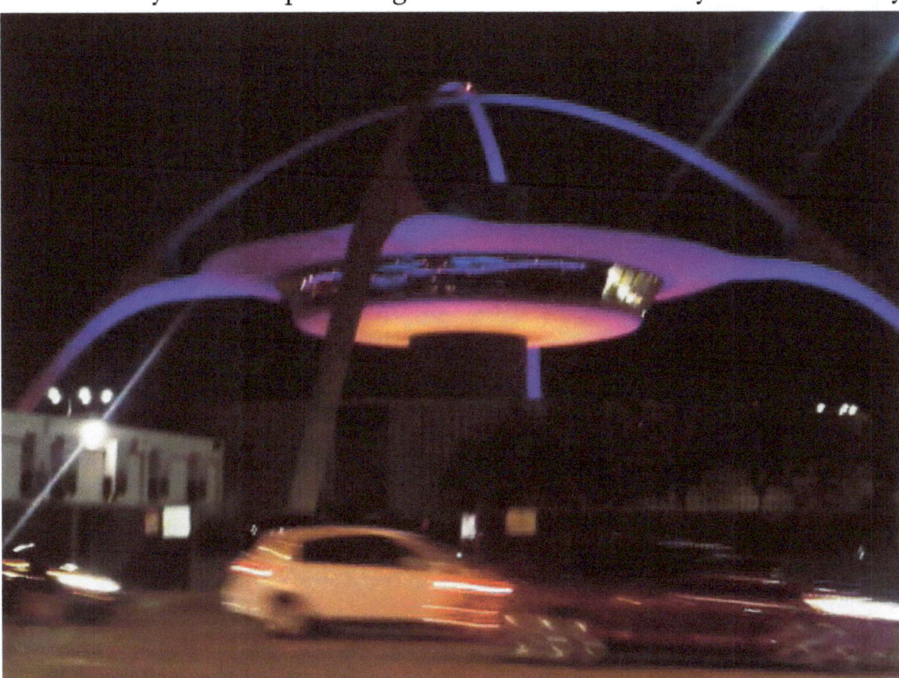

photograph by Kym Ghee

After a real long time it was over and people clap and up out their seats and crowd away and I look at Rudy and Rudy looks at me and we're both still here so what happened to the end of the world? I ask Cassandra about this because Ramona's still going on about she knows what words mean in Yiddish and Cassandra says it was the ringcicle, she says this part of the ringcicle's the end of the world. I say, "Oh, ringcicle, uh-huh," and Cassandra nods and gets lipstick out her purse and puts it on without a mirror. I say the end of the world's just like before the end of the world, I say wasn't there supposed to be a explosion or something? Donnell says, "Ringcicle, sure, it's the bomb," and I know he don't know what it is either, but we all get ice cream at the good place, which they don't have ringcicles and never heard of them, so how about that? And we wait for the crowd to thin out and we say thanks and it was great and see you soon to everybody and they go off for the F but we go for the Q. Rudy's asleep on his feet by the time a Q train pulls in and I'm not much better, tell the truth, and we ride and we ride all the way back to Union Square. I find a paper and read up on the Mets 'cause the end of the world's just like before the end of the world and now I got all this catch-up to do but it's hard to keep my eyes open and I figure the Mets aren't going to change after the end of the world on account of they don't change for nothing, I'll read up on them tomorrow. From Union Square we walk and we walk all the way home. "Last one up the stair's a rotten egg!" says Rudy, but I beat him to our door even though he's got the head start on me. I got to hide the laundry quarters before Rudy grabs them, if he gets hold of that money he'll stop the next ice cream truck to try and buy every kid on our block a ringcicle.

Suicide Tour

Marty Thau

Suicide, the seminally important and confrontational duo consisting of vocalist Alan Vega and electronic musician Martin Rev, formed in 1970 and have been active intermittently since that time.

* * *

A FEW MONTHS AFTER THE RELEASE OF Suicide's debut album, I received a telegram from the promoters of the 3rd International Science Fiction Festival to be held in Metz, France, in late May '78. They asked if the duo would be interested in appearing as the Festival's sole musical attraction. All their expenses would be paid, plus they would receive a minimal fee and co-headline with keynote speaker Frank Herbert, author of the science fiction novel *Dune*. It was a timely offer because John Peel, then England's leading underground DJ, and the British weeklies *Time Out*, *NME*, *Melody Maker* and *Sounds*, were praising the album enthusiastically. Not only that, but the engagement would bring Red Star's masterful prodigies overseas at a minimal expense.

I passed the information on to Bronze Records, Red Star's London-based European distributor, and they helped spread the news that Suicide were coming to Europe. Shortly afterward, the duo were booked to open for Elvis Costello on his first tour of Europe, and for a series of thirty shows opening for the Clash that would take Suicide through the whole of England. We couldn't have asked for better exposure, because Costello and the Clash were both sizzling hot and major Suicide fans.

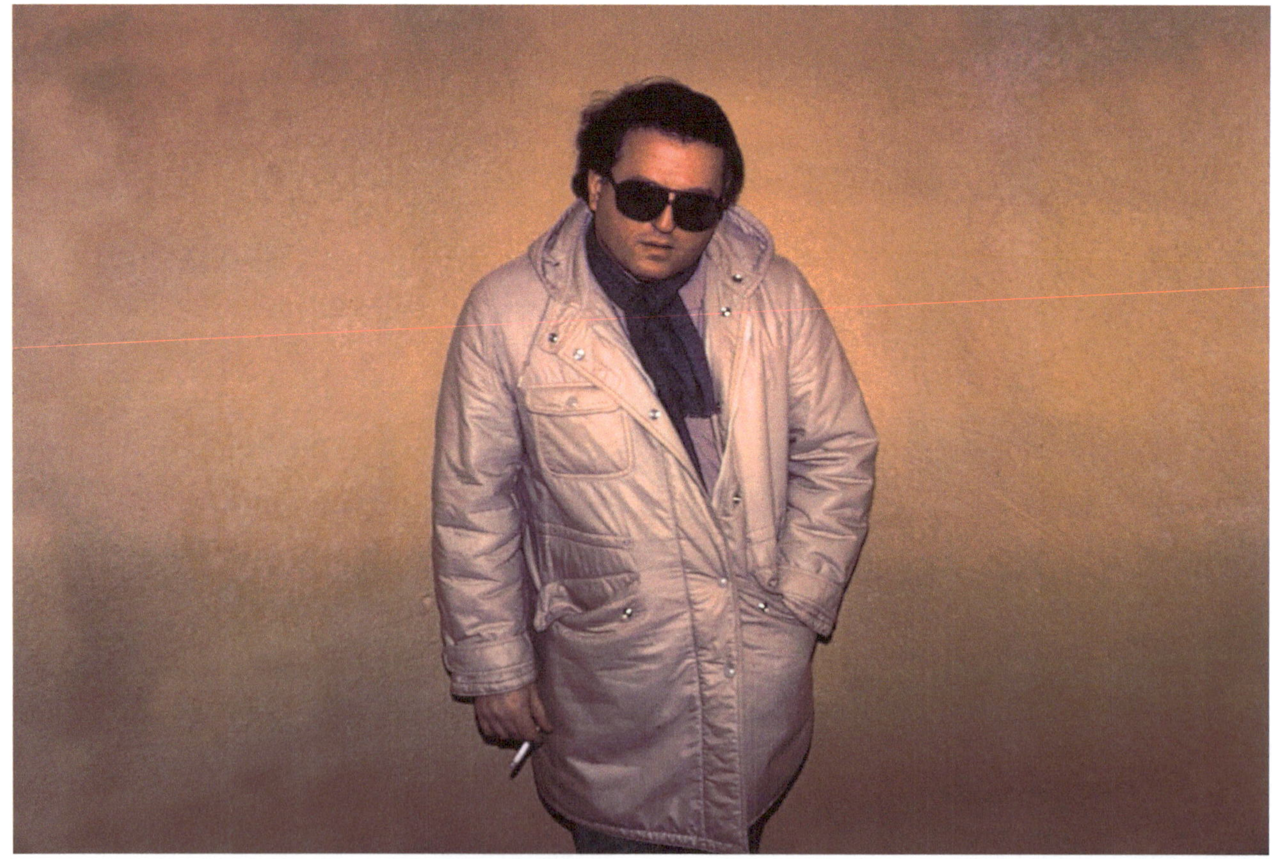

Suicide's tour with Costello carved a swath through the continent and kicked off in Brussels at the Anciennes Belgique Theatre on June 16, 1978. Audience reactions were unlike anything seen before in Europe.

Cocky, wired and adrenalized, Vega didn't take long to alienate the crowd. You could sense the confusion resonating through the audience, who had come to see Elvis Costello but were being subjected to the full impact of Suicide's hypnotic down-and-dirty culture shock. Vega chose to ignore the shouts of attendees who had never experienced such a strange, guitar-free outfit before, which is why he was caught off-guard when a belligerent audience member jumped onstage and, to the cheers of the bewildered, ripped the microphone out of his hands. Half the audience started to chant what sounded like garbled Belgian farm anthems, while the other half applauded Suicide's irrepressible passion.

On any given night, in any venue in any town, anything not nailed down would inevitably come flying through the air in Suicide's general direction. In Glasgow, Scotland, an axe was actually thrown at Vega and barely missed hitting him.

As was the case with the New York Dolls, it was obvious you either embraced Suicide wholeheartedly or loathed them vehemently. There was no in-between. This hate/love reaction was undeniably mystifying but in time would inspire many forceful disagreements and debates in the rock press.

After Suicide's surreal performance, our New York contingent was told that a still-provoked audience had attacked the stage before Costello could even begin his set. The riot gendarmes had been called and soon the irritating odor of tear gas filled the auditorium. We didn't need any more incentives to vacate the premises. Alan, Rev, Roy Trakin, Red Star's Minister of Information, Miriam and I ran down a corridor adjacent to the stage to a side exit leading to an alleyway, where we piled into a vehicle waiting for us and sped out of there as fast as we could. That night, Suicide got a taste of what they would be forced to endure on upcoming dates with Costello and the Clash.

Later that evening, our New York contingent were at a late-night after-hours club when they were greeted warmly by Costello and his band members, who invited them to celebrate Suicide's victorious invasion of Europe. That first show would set the tone for the entire tour, which I dubbed "Blood '78."

Howard Thompson, who had been assigned to chaperone the duo throughout the tour, recorded their Brussels appearance on his Sony cassette player for his label. The recording soon became an official vinyl bootleg which *NME* readers could order for free from Bronze Records. The performance/riot, given the name "23 Minutes Over Brussels" by Roy Trakin and often touted as Suicide's "Metallic KO," was also included in the Mute reissue of Suicide's debut LP in 1998 and has since become a coveted collector's item.

As Thompson later wrote in his sleeve notes to Suicide's *Live 1977-78,* a six-CD box set that was released by the U.K.'s Blast First Petite Records in July 2008: "On any given night, in any venue in any town, anything not nailed down would inevitably come flying through the air in Suicide's general direction. In Glasgow, Scotland, an axe was actually thrown at Vega and barely missed hitting him."

In Paris, Suicide delivered a sizzling twenty-minute set, the climax of which involved Vega's

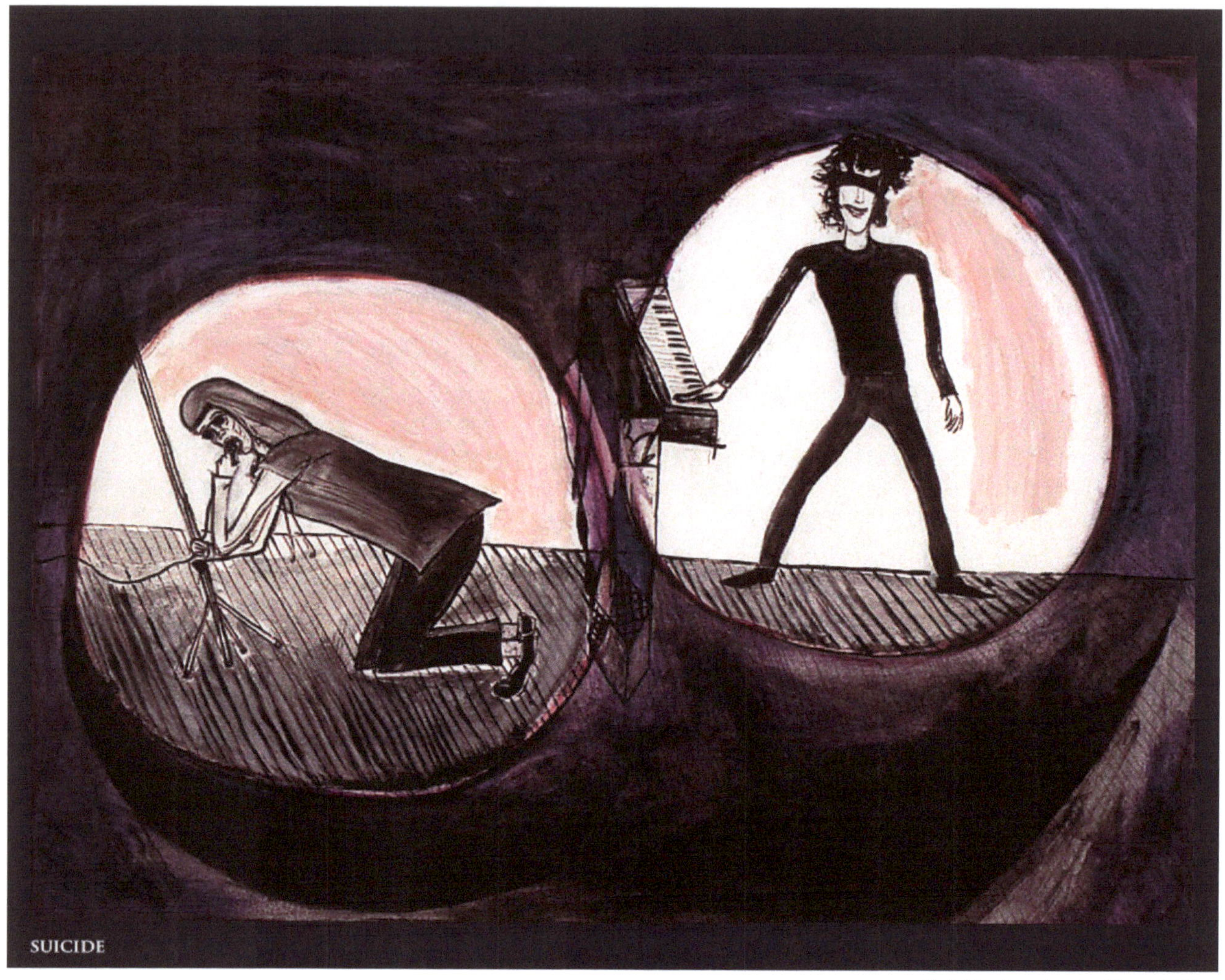

Suicide, drawing by David West

taunting the French for the distinctive body odor and hirsute armpits of their whores. By the end of the tour, Vega was offering German fans his perspective on their supposed racist and anti-Semitic neo-Nazi tendencies.

The very next day, Suicide flew to England to join the Clash tour in Leicester at Granby Hall. At the Music Machine shows in London's Camden Town, Clash fans drenched Vega and his newly cleaned purple suit with a rain of spit when he hit the stage and moved toward the solitary center microphone. As the opening strains of "Ghost Rider" filled the venue, the outpouring increased with a relentless barrage of coins, bottles, and whatever else the audience could lay their hands on. But despite Vega's pleasure at being on the receiving end of hostile provocation, on the night of that fourth sold-out show at the Music Machine in London, he and Rev finally won over the audience and received an ovation and call for an encore.

Expecting to laugh and snicker at the expense of two primal weirdos, the audience was surprised by the level of active involvement which Suicide's presentation fed them. Accustomed to dealing with tentative, uncertain audiences, the band seemed to grow more dominant visibly and, as one song pounded into another, began to turn the corner. The audience was being told to make use of their dormant imaginations.

In Blackburn, the local police were hoping to arrest the Clash for drug possession, but the support crew were too clever to be compromised by the over-confident *gendarmes* and were alert to such obvious maneuvers. When the police finally realized they weren't going to garner any national headlines arresting the Clash, they shifted their attention to Suicide. Turning up a small amount of what they believed to be a hash-like substance in Rev's personal belongings, they arrested the duo on suspicion of drug possession, but the charges were dismissed in court after tests showed the substance was a seasoning. It seems that Rev had tried to purchase a small amount of pot in Amsterdam, but the dealer had ripped him off and sold him oregano!

Howard Thompson, testifying as a character witness, described Suicide's artistic importance and portrayed them as choirboys. Fortunately, the judge accepted his earnest spiel and the fine of a mere 400 pounds was levied against Suicide, which was paid subsequently by Bronze's London office. As if that wasn't enough, Suicide came under attack from the punk establishment in the form of Johnny Lydon, who opined in the *New Musical Express* that Suicide's single, "Cheree," was like "Je t'aime . . . moi non plus" with tape hiss.

The entire series of shows with Suicide supporting the Clash are now regarded as nigh-mythical events which brought about some of the most extreme abuse any music group has ever suffered. It also spawned a legion of admirers who then formed their own bands after witnessing the power of Red Star's dynamic duo. Primal Scream's Bobby Gillespie, in attendance at more than one of the shows, has called Suicide "one of the greatest rock & roll bands ever," while pop giants Bono, Bruce Springsteen, Michael Stipe, Ric Ocasek and Depeche Mode have publicly concurred.

By the end of the Clash tour, Suicide had won over enough fans to headline their own sold-out show at London's historic Marquee Club, where the audience demanded an unexpected and rare encore. A triumphant Berlin headlining appearance closed out the campaign, and thus was born the Suicide cult that continues to thrive to this day.

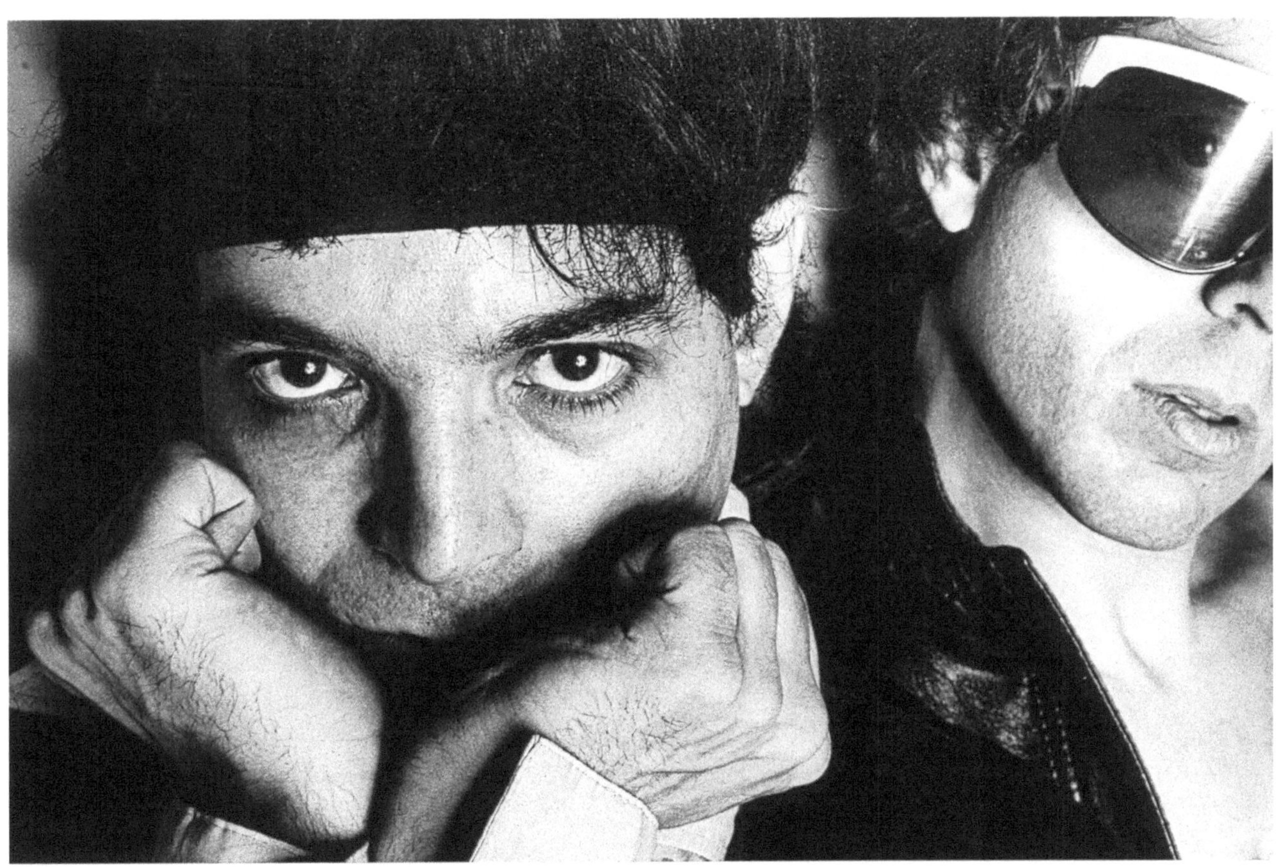

Sodomy Is a Threat to National Security

Jesús Ángel García

COSTUMES

On Saturday morning at the KKK meetup, the hooded outfits came in a variety of flavors, from milky white to tea green. One guy wore a Confederate flag that made him look like a Southern-fried Statue of Liberty. His headband bore the slogan RAHOWA. Cyrus said that stood for "Racial Holy War." Half the marchers covered their faces. The ones who didn't had fugly moustaches, their shrunken heads topped with the standard wizard hat or a checkered hunting cap, which tended to clash with their linens.

All of them were Boy Scouts, their uniforms modified with badges, swastikas, iron crosses or the popular W beneath a haloed crown in a circle of WBWs ("Whiter Brighter World"). Another common motto was "Sic Semper Tyrannis" (Thus Always to Tyrants), a nod to John Wilkes Booth's shout-out before capping the Great Emancipator at *Beach Blanket Babylon*.

Gay Pride the next day was a more colorful affair. The standout fashions: rainbow-scaled leotards, radioactive farmgirl frocks, and fluorescent goddess gowns, elaborate headdresses of yellow, red and orange feathers. The players: sequined belly dancers, buff leather daddies, barkers in jackets with shining epaulets, bare-chested body builders in red-white-and-blue Speedos. The genders were sometimes mix-matched beyond recognition.

At first, this made me uncomfortable, but by nightfall, I had warmed up to the notion. Perhaps gender's as much a farce as ideals of perfection or the games we play with God. Opting in or out is a contract with oneself, subject to fad, whim, intestinal fortitude. Masks and face paint veiled identities, evoking the fancy of fairy tales or animation come to life. On Bebe's suggestion, I wore a purple bouffant wig, mime makeup and giant swirly sunglasses to foil any First Church brethren who happened into the crossfire.

Bebe dressed up in pink fur earmuffs, choker, bikini top, mini skirt, bracelets and anklets. Her bare arms, legs and midriff showed off her gym-toned body and the sharp curling abstractions inked on her skin. She designed them herself, called them The Path. To me, they appeared to be barbed wire and jungle vines. To complete her kitty metamorphosis, she'd given herself a black button nose with dainty whiskers that looked like sideways teardrops.

Aside from his plastic crown of thorns, Cyrus dressed down, shirtless, flexing the wings on his back, wearing only tight jeans and his trademark gator boots. His torso was taut and tan, the arrowhead above his J.C. belt buckle an invitation.

When he first told me I not only had to go with him and Bebe to this gig but get out in the street with them, I asked if he was gay.

"Homophobic much?" he said.

"No!" I remember saying too loudly, too quickly. Maybe I was trying to convince myself. It wasn't that I ever had a problem with homosexuality as a biological condition or lifestyle choice. I just never knew anyone personally who shaded that way until I met Bebe, so I hadn't given it much thought. When Cyrus put it in my face, I felt uneasy. I wanted to know where he stood. Just to know.

SIGNS

There was such preaching from all sides, we might as well have been at church. Chief among the Klan banners: *White Is Right*, *This Land Is Our Land*, *Now's the Hour for White Power!* There were cartoon pics on posterboards of Mexicans, Arabs and blacks with captions like "Ax the Wetbacks," "Go Home, Mañuel," the familiar "A Friend Indeed Is a Towel Head That Bleeds" and "Bury the Mud Races!" Among the group's supporters lined along the sidewalk: *Buy American*, *ICE ICE Baby*, *There's a Border for a Reason*, *Harboring Aliens Smells like Treason*. From our counterperch on the opposite side of the street: *Hate Is Not Great*, *We Are All God's Creation*, *Aliens Do Not Exist*.

I don't remember raising any signs myself, but I did respond to chants for "White power!" with "Mice glower?" and "More golden showers, less baby powder!" That riled the hoodies, who were so moved, they tore off their face masks to better scream at us, their pale cheeks going red like boils on the bum of Frosty the Snowman.

At the Gay Pride rally, the rainbows were splashed with messages lifted from song lyrics: *Peace Love & Understanding*, *Equal Rights & Justice*, *Give Peace a Chance*. There were the biblical appropriations *Love Your Neighbor as Yourself* and *Who Among You Can Cast the First Stone?* The haters fired back: petty (*Unnatural Unclean*, *Bad Bad Bad*), brutal (*AIDS Is Natural Selection*), apocalyptic (*Repent Today or Pay the Price Tomorrow*) and absurd (*Sodomy Is a Threat to National Security*).

I didn't advertise at this gathering either. I thought of myself as an active spectator, a passive participant. For me, these events were high times with friends, a chance to goof in public and maybe meet some girls. Like I said, I'm not political—and I'm not gay—so I didn't feel right waving somebody else's flag.

RIGHT, LEFT . . . LEFT RIGHT LEFT

Both demonstrations took place in the same part of town, starting on Jordan Drive, about a mile out from city hall, winding onto the streets that circled the seat of local government, convening in Peter & Paul Park, a small square of green outside the mayor's office. The Klan processional was led by a pointy-headed knight on a white horse trailed by his foot soldiers. Spearheading Gay Pride was a team of pony boys, saddled and harnessed, silver bits in their mouths. At the reins, a king and queen in swapped gender roles steered an outsized red wagon straight down the roads of Gethsemane.

The white supremacists raised Confederate and W flags, while stars-and-stripes and rainbows flew the following day. The Klansmen marched with the discipline of a militia, lapping around the government building before settling in for hate speech at the plaza. Dykes and fairies and their straight allies, advocates for broadmindedness and equality like myself, rolled down the street on sparkly floats, bikes and unicycles. The rest of us ambled along or flitted like fireflies around the costumed vehicles.

As you would expect, brother, I walked normally.

BODY COUNT

There were more folks on the sidelines than in the streets at each demonstration. The KKK marchers totaled no more than three dozen, while the Gay Proud probably maxed out at a couple hundred. Nazi sympathizers, the ones I talked to anyhow, argued that they were "God-fearing Christians, tolerant of individual differences and in no way racist, but the

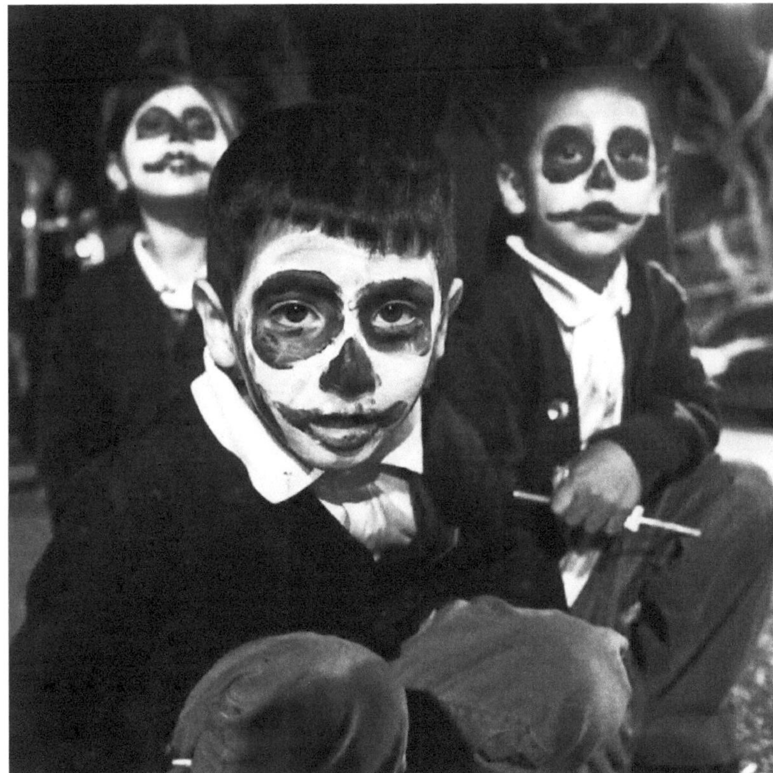

photograph by N.D. Koster

scourge of illegal immigration" had brought them out "to defend the American way of life." Their numbers matched ours on the opposite side of the avenue at about a thousand or so, all told. A sizable crowd, but not overwhelming.

The Pride parade was far more out of hand, with maybe ten times as many counterdemonstrators: Bible thumpers one and all, most of them hysterical, as if the Wrath of God would smite the whole town for the shameless exhibitionism of a few immoralists. Some must have showed for kicks, to gawk at the outfits, jeer at the queers. The majority likely turned out under orders from their Lord and Savior as conveyed from the pulpits of the region's megachurches.

To my surprise, our First Church reverend rejected the bandwagon. He believed ignoring the rally would send a more appropriate message, not giving credence to what he called "perversion akin to pornography."

POLITICS

THE WHITE SUPREMACIST agenda seemed so out of touch with the times it was laughable. Outside the shooting range, the racism I'd observed since moving to the Dirty South was largely contained, integrated into daily routines, as if segregation by skin color was a choice agreed upon by all parties. Cyrus explained how most folks leaned toward their own kind to dial down the potential for trouble with the law. All anybody wanted, he said, was to do their own thing without interference from the busybodies who would never understand "the culture of selective kinship." Even among the counterdemonstrators, there were divisions between blacks, whites and Latinos. Bebe's wide-angle snapshot of the crowd looks like a neatly divided, triple-layer cake of chocolate, vanilla and mocha.

The political issues at the Klan march were immigration policy, border security and the rights of U.S.-born citizens versus the rights of immigrants ("legal" and "illegal"). There was a lot of poofed-up talk about jobs, schools and healthcare, and how the taxpayer was footing the bill for an "alien invasion."

Even though I don't identify as Latino, I get it that Mexican blood flows through my veins. But I'm not sure what this means, brother. I know nothing of mom's side of the family. She said she was an only child, both of her parents dead. I still find this hard to believe. I've never been south of the border. I don't speak Spanish. Burritos funk up my insides. Mariachi is wack. But I have to admit, hearing all that trash laid on the Latinos made me ball up my fists.

At the Pride rally, there were calls for same-sex marriage, though these seemed like token gestures with no hope of changing the system. The opposition had public support by a wide margin. Feeling their power, the holy rollers got missionary, collecting signatures to place an anti-sodomy measure on the local ballot. This would buck the recent Supreme Court ruling that such laws were unconstitutional. "God's law," they said, "is the only one that matters." Their hue and cry against choice in the bedroom made me want to fuck them all up the ass.

VIOLENCE

IT SEEMED LIKE every cop in the county and gangs of state troopers had been summoned to keep the peace. Armed with clubs, tear gas, stun guns and high-powered rifles that shot rubber bullets, they formed human barricades to separate the factions and enable the demonstrators to pass by. I overheard "fuckin freaks" at each event, the consensus among the law enforcers, though they did their jobs without incident.

A couple of Nazi youths were arrested for assaulting a mixed-race kid during one of the golden shower chants. A Klansman was pelted with beans while burning a Mexican flag. When he argued with police—he could have had an eye poked out!—he was cited for lighting a fire on public property without a permit. A half-dozen or so Christian Crusaders were detained but later released without charges, a local blog reported the next day, after hurling what they said was holy water at boys in chaps on one of the floats. A church whose members littered the street with pamphlets on cleaning up the city was fined.

Otherwise, the confrontations were limited to big noise, posturing and threats of God's Almighty Wrath. Just another weekend in Gethsemane.

Interview: Fred Frith

The Editors

THREE SENSITIVE SKIN EDITORS—FLUFFY Schwartz, B. Kold and Sir Reginald Brathwaite—had a chat with legendary musician and composer Fred Frith. We asked him some good questions, and some (or so he apparently thought) pedantic ones. But that's how we roll. Fred's answers were always interesting...

SS: Has having a psychologist for a brother affected your approach to music? Has the study of psychology influenced your understanding of composition, improvisation, performance and collaboration?

FRED FRITH: I have not studied psychology, though I did go through an extended period of Jungian therapy more than 20 years ago. Trying to understand oneself better seems to me a useful attribute for an artist, or anyone else for that matter. My brother has influenced my approach to everything, not by being a neuroscientist, but by being a wonderful role model in the realms of music and art, and by his intense curiosity and rich appreciation of life's absurdities!

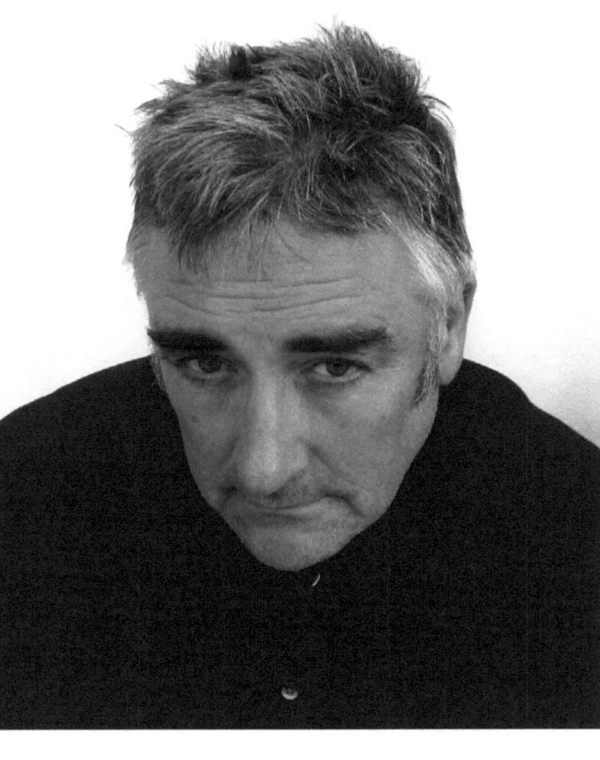

SS: In 1979, you wrote an article for *NME,* "Great Rock Solos of our Time." Have you changed your mind about any of those guys, based on what they've done since? What rock guitar players of today do you admire?

FF: I haven't read those articles in many years, but I'm fairly sure my subjects would hold up to scrutiny! Current rock players? Nels Kline. Ava Mendoza. Alee Karim. Gilles Laval.

SS: Any other currently working musicians or composers you admire? Any special favorites in improvised music?

FF: Far too many to name all of them. But of those you may not know: Annie Lewandowski, Katharina Weber, Lucas Niggli, Bérangère Maximin, Eduard Perraud, Paolo Angeli, Camel Zekri, Jason Hoopes, Jordan Glenn.

SS: Chamber or contemporary classical music?

FF: Not my area of expertise. But I like the animated notation school of composers, like Steini Gunnarsson and Ryan Ross Smith.

SS: At last count, you've played on some 410 albums. Which stand out as your personal favorites, the ones you feel are most enjoyable and/or most important?

FF: Wouldn't know where to begin. I'm generally more concerned with what I'm doing now! [Editor's Note: If you're not familiar with Fred's ouevre, we suggest starting with *Guitar Solos, Gravity,* and *Step Across the Border.*]

SS: What are some of your favorite albums or compositions, the pieces that were most influential to your body of work and the history of music?

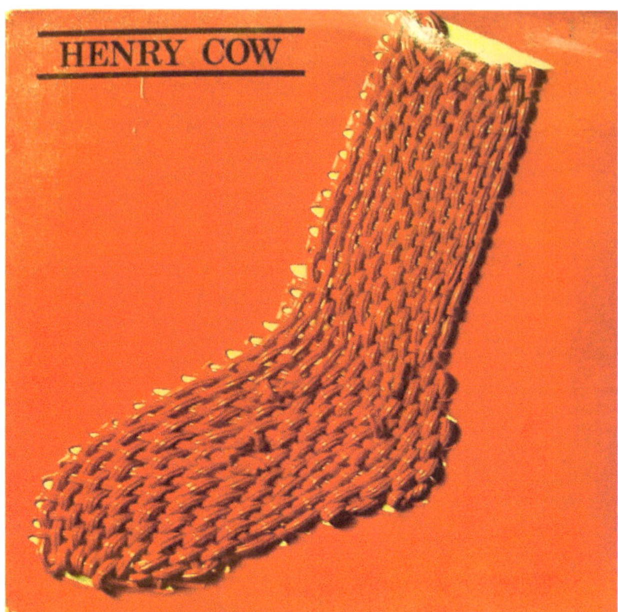

Henry Cow, *In Praise of Learning*, 1975

FF: The biggest influences on what I do are the people I've been lucky enough to work with, whether they're the members of Henry Cow and Skeleton Crew, performers like Evelyn Glennie or John Zorn, or the members of my current band, Cosa Brava. I'm often very influenced by my own failures, and you don't get to hear those!

SS: Has teaching composition changed your approach to performance (or vice versa)?

FF: My approach changes all the time, based on everything I'm going through, whether teaching, not teaching, composing, performing, cooking, talking, arguing, watching birds, going to movies, or reading books.

SS: Have you been influenced by any of your students?

FF: I hope so.

SS: Has your tenure at Mills College and later focus on classical composition led to any reevaluation of your earlier work?

FF: I don't really do "classical" composition, and I've been composing on paper since I was 14. Whenever possible I compose what I hear for musicians who want to play what I write. Some of them are classically trained, and some of them aren't. I am constantly re-evaluating everything I do.

SS: Do you see the earlier work as preparation for this stage or as work with a completely different set of aims and accomplishments?

FF: Not in any conscious sense, and not beyond the general idea that everything that you do leads in some way to everything else. In general, my aim has always been to make sense of what I hear, and that hasn't changed.

SS: You recently performed *Gravity* in its entirety. Was that enjoyable? Any plans to do it again, or something similar?

FF: It was wonderful. I can't wait to give it another shot.

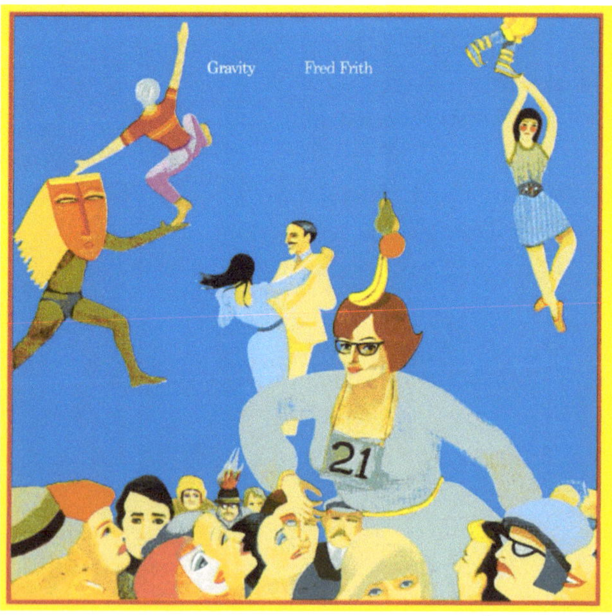

Gravity, 1980

SS: Do you draw a distinction between your fully notated chamber music and free improvisation?

FF: Of course.

SS: Do you think of them as separate and

compartmentalized?

FF: Of course not.

SS: Despite your early musical training and experience, you graduated from college with a BA in literature and got your MA in the same subject. Why did you choose that path, and does it have a bearing on decision to write lyrics for what could easily have been purely instrumental bands?

FF: It was the only path open to me at the time. I failed in everything else, and I had no formal training in music and would not have been admitted to a music program. Much as I love words, I hate writing lyrics and usually try to find someone else to do it.

SS: Moving to New York was greatly freeing for you—what's it been like to move to the Bay Area? Do you miss NY? Do you miss England? Any comments on the Bay Area music scene?

FF: My community stopped being identifiably centered in one geographical location a long time ago. I'm in New York every year and still have deep personal connections there. London, too, and many other cities. Lately, I've been spending a lot of time in Copenhagen. I tend to go where I'm invited, and the community I feel that I belong to is always evolving and mutating. The Bay Area scene has always been vibrant and exciting and I've been coming here regularly since my first concert in San Francisco in 1979, so moving here was not a great leap into the unknown. There's a lot going on here, though I'm perhaps more drawn to the younger generation of creative musicians, because many of them stay on in the area after they graduate from Mills and I'm excited to see them develop. All I can say is that the scene is as vibrant and exciting as it's ever been, and yet has an almost shocking lack of local media interest or support. If this were NY in 1978 or Chicago in the early '90s, we would be the center of gravity for American creative music right now, but the media are so unadventurous they've never noticed, and there simply aren't enough decent venues to take chances and try to build up the scene. Thank goodness for the ones that DO exist!

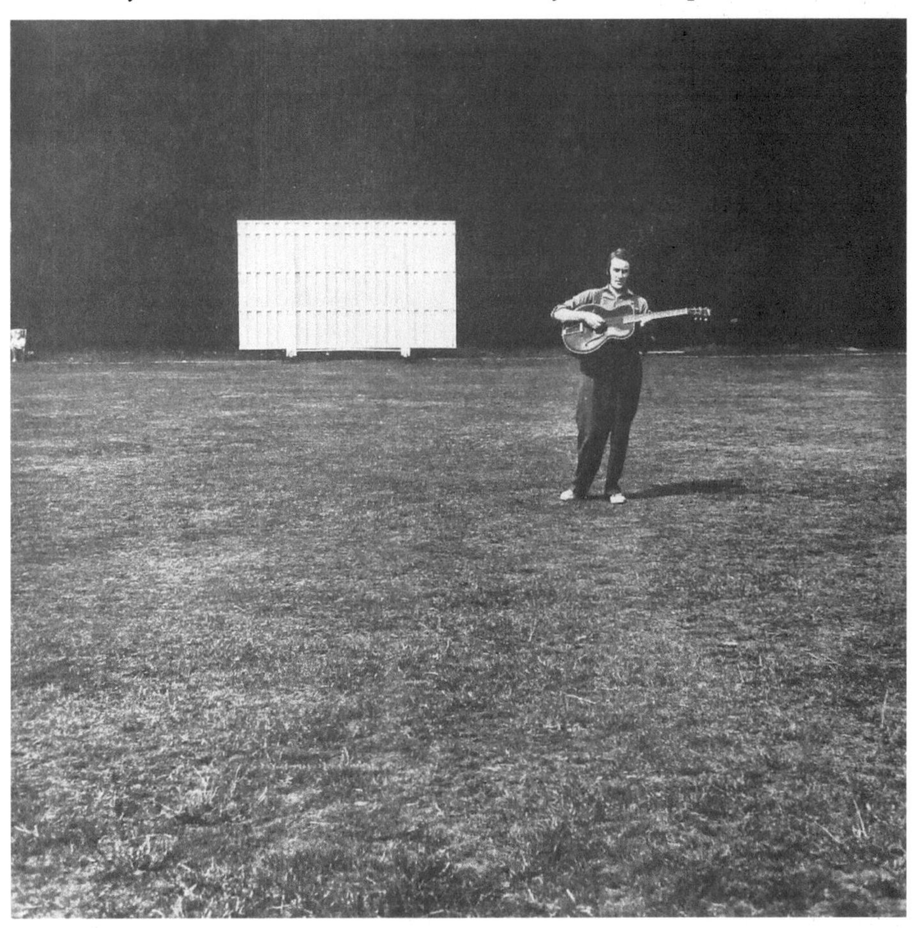

Guitar Solos, 1974

SS: Did you ever feel lonely having a bookish background on tours with bandmates trained purely as musicians? How did the study of literature affect your approach to music? Did it affect the way you communicated with other artists?

FF: Are you kidding me? My study of literature has been almost entirely irrelevant to my social life as a musician, and the people I work with are frequently

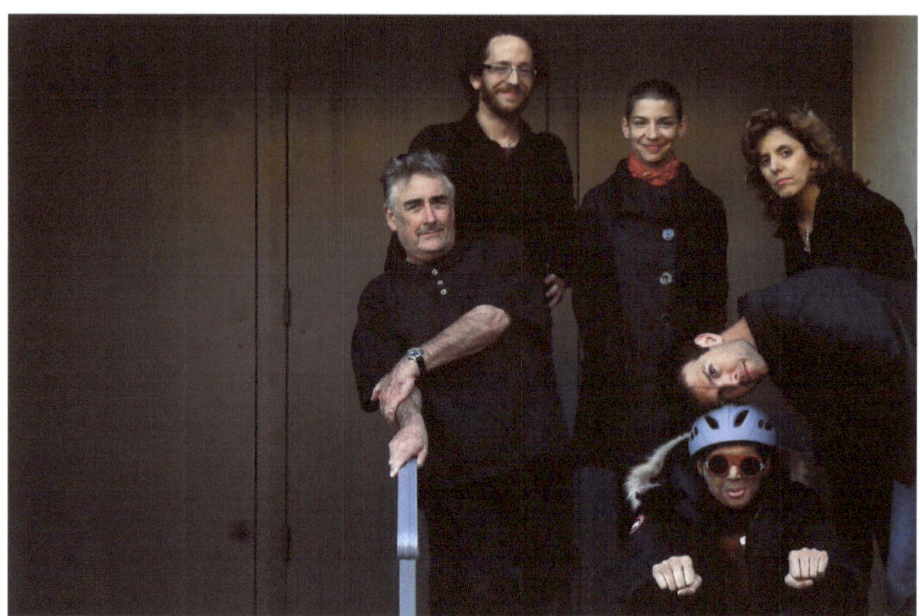

Fred Frith and Cosa Brava

some of the most well-read, articulate, open-minded, inquisitive and fascinating folks I know. The only time I feel lonely is when I'm traveling by myself, which seems logical to me!

SS: Sometimes your approach (and that of your musicians) seems to change from album to album. How would you prep a new player for work as diverse as yours?

FF: I work together with musicians to realize specific projects. The diversity of my work is not something we discuss. I generally try to work with players who are able to handle all the angles. It's more a question of how I prep myself to work with them.

SS: Over the course of your career, you've played with an incredible variety of musicians—Zeena Parkins, Mike Patton, Brian Eno, the Ensemble Modern, Ikue Mori, Tom Cora, the Residents, Bill Laswell, John Zorn and the Arditti Quartet. Did you change your overview and approach drastically to work with any of these vastly different musicians? Which collaborators stand out as your favorites?

FF: I like to challenge myself by working in situations where I can learn something I didn't already know. Maybe in order to really get a sense of that it would be good to add a few names that are maybe not so much in the Anglo-American new music "mainstream": Babazula, Stevie Wishart, Keiji Haino, Concerto Köln, Wu Fei, Mart Soo, Daniela Cattivelli, Lucia Recio– I've learned so much from working with musicians like these, and I take any opportunity I can to seek such collaborations out.

SS: There's an unusually diverse range of styles and approaches to writing, arranging and improvising in your body of work, and yet it all sounds like you somehow. When collaborating, do you switch between stylistic palettes or approaches in your head, or do you believe in the idea of musicians staying in character? How mutable is your idea of contrast between players in an ensemble?

FF: Why wouldn't it sound like me? It IS me! I'm generally trying to wrestle with material in a particular context with particular parameters and particular players. What emerges is the result of a process. I

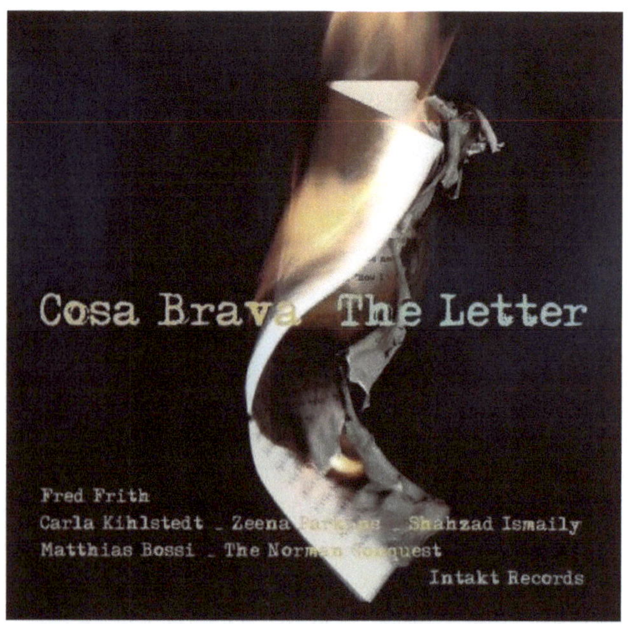

Cosa Brava, *The Letter, 2012*

guide the process by trying to balance my original ideas with what the players bring to the table. Luckily it isn't always the way I expect it to be. Choosing the right players is the single most important decision. Sometimes they choose themselves, like Kaethe Hostetter, who wanted to play violin in the Gravity show and "presented her credentials" as it were! That was awesome!

SS: Zeena Parkins's work on Cosa Brava's *The Letter* (Intakt Records) is very different from that on *Traffic Continues II.* Do you tend to ask your musicians to try different approaches? Do you prefer them to enter into the work without preconceptions?

I'm generally trying to wrestle with material in a particular context with particular parameters and particular players. What emerges is the result of a process. I guide the process by trying to balance my original ideas with what the players bring to the table. Luckily it isn't always the way I expect it to be.

FF: I've known Zeena for more than 30 years. She was in my bands Skeleton Crew and Keep the Dog in the '80s and '90s respectively. I'm well aware of the vast range of her talents as harpist, pianist, accordionist, experimenter, composer, inventor, improviser. I would want to work with Z in any situation that required flexibility, a broad skillset, a fabulous work ethic, and a strong intuitive understanding of what's required. When the Ensemble Modern commission came along, it was a chance to invite her to play her first instrument, an opportunity that doesn't come along very often. It was also the first time that the EM had featured women soloists (Ikue Mori being the other). As for different approaches, we try different approaches if what we're doing doesn't seem to be working. And I prefer players to "enter into a work" in whatever way seems productive to them.

SS: How conscious were the folk and Celtic elements of The Letter, especially in the violin parts?

FF: I was awake when I wrote them, if that's what you mean.

SS: What about the elements of pastiche that seem to hearken back to Henry Cow (such as the baroque sequence of fifths in *For Lars Hollmer)?*

FF: Owes as much to Victor Jara or Kurt Weill as it does to Baroque music. And in any case what I love about Lars Hollmer's work is that he made melodies that seemed like you'd known them all your life, but which were also personal enough that they were obviously his. That was the quality I was looking for, not so much imitation as invocation. Lars was a dear friend and a huge influence and I miss him.

SS: You've collaborated with Iva Bittová in the past, who shares your background in Eastern European folk music as well as classical music—do you seek out that sort of background in collaborators and performers of your music?

FF: I like working with collaborators who share a broad sense of the possibilities and are not bound to a single approach. And I like improvising with musicians who don't define themselves as "improvisers".

SS: Your early influences included many kinds of world and Eastern-European folk music—a rare set of influences for a Western musician in those days. How directly did your early interest in world and folk music impact on your accompaniment to her voice?

FF: No idea. I wasn't thinking about it particularly.

SS: Do you think of it as accompaniment or something else?

FF: See above.

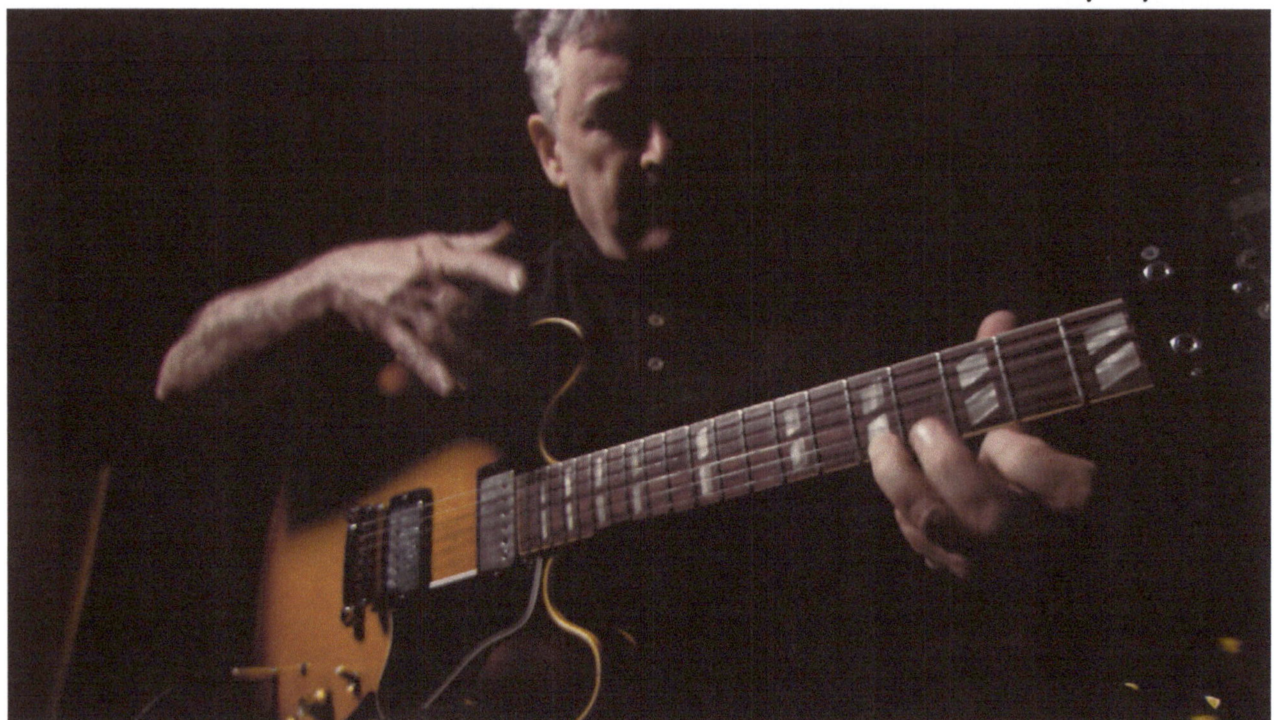

SS: There are lots of unison lines performed by voices, guitars and violins instruments. This suggests you might be aiming for a verbal but not necessarily a vocal sound: The voices of verbal instruments. Is there a connection between the voices of instruments and the content of verbal expression?

FF: I'm not sure if I know what you're talking about. Which lines are you referring to? The best example that I know of understanding instruments as voices (outside of the blues) is René Lussier's *Trésor de la Langue*. More than simply a masterpiece, it changes our understanding of the musicality of language.

SS: On *The Letter*, but also on many of your other albums, the use of accordion, and of pitched and higher sounds in the percussion and synths, gives the violin and guitar a magical sound that reminds me of *Lick My Decals off, Baby*. There's a glow to the parts. Do you think of certain sounds as shimmering, glowing, or nacreous?

FF: I had to look that up! And no, not particularly. We're just trying to make it sound good.

TO LISTEN TO A SELECTION OF TRACKS BY FRED, GO HERE:
www.sensitiveskinmagazine.com/fred-frith

WATCH THE AWARD-WINNING DOCUMENTARY *STEP ACROSS THE BORDER* HERE:
http://youtu.be/WahnZ1HcW00

Photographs

Chris Bava

Arriving in Tijuana after over a decade of heroin abuse in a past life, I felt the garish lights of Tijuana's *zona de tolerancia,* or North Zone, beckoning. I was fascinated by their resonance, and the street life, brimming with pathos, quickly made *la zona norte* my favorite part of town. The challenge of taking a camera to *El Bordo,* the river bottom that runs along the border between Mexico and the U.S., where an estimated 2,000 homeless drug addicted US deportees live, was irresistible. I would drive along Via Rapide, known as the "most dangerous road in TJ," and look at the shadowy figures crouched along the river bank, or on the highway meridian, openly cooking up and shooting heroin. I became determined to gain access. Everyone I asked told me it was too risky. One day I decided to chance it. I noticed two guys poised at the edge of the highway about to daringly dodge traffic to reach the river bank on the other side. I flagged them down: "Hey, you wanna make a little cash? Let me take some photos." So began a long, interesting friendship with the people of *Zona Norte.*

—*Chris Bava*

As we were going to press, we learned that Chris died in a car accident, along with his wife and brother, early in the morning of October 21, 2012. This issue is dedicated to his memory.

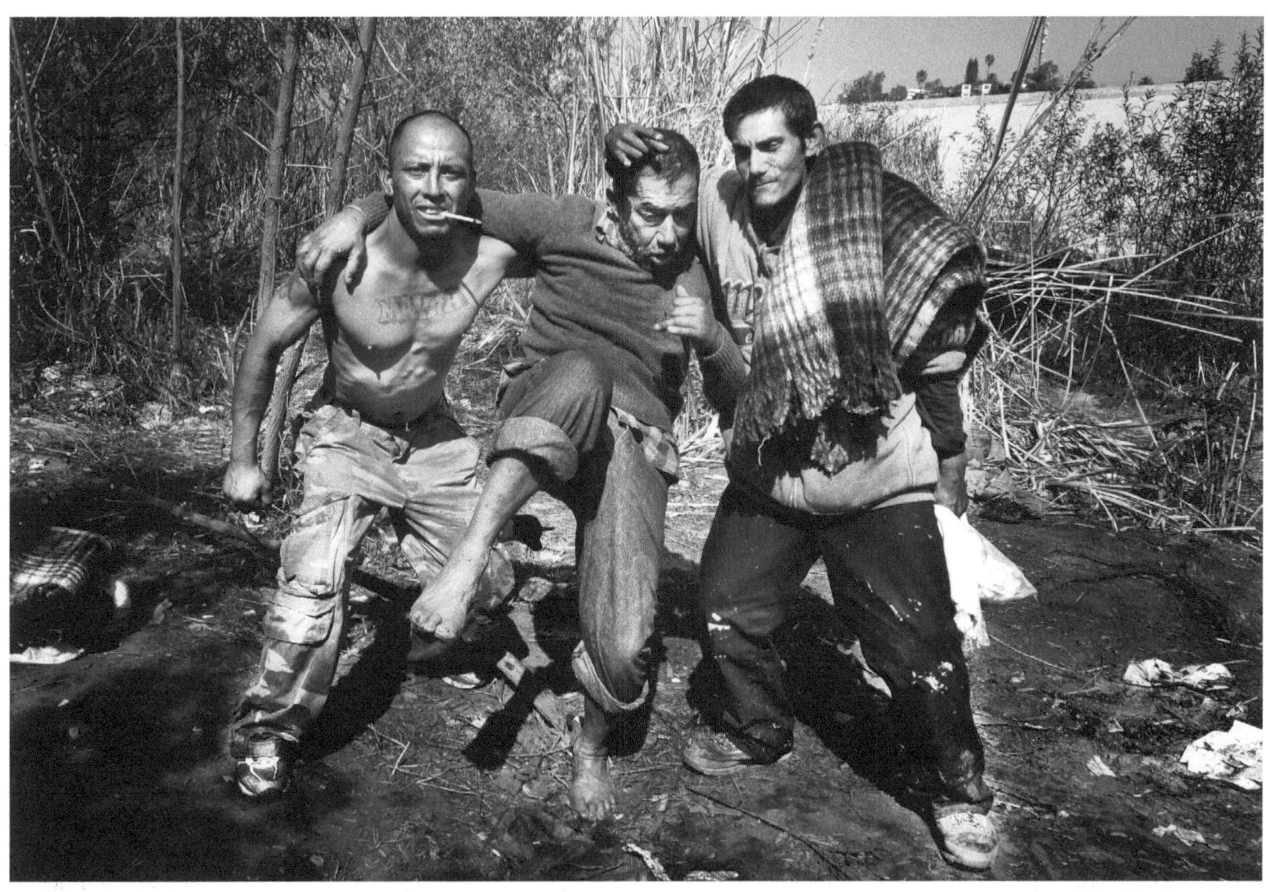

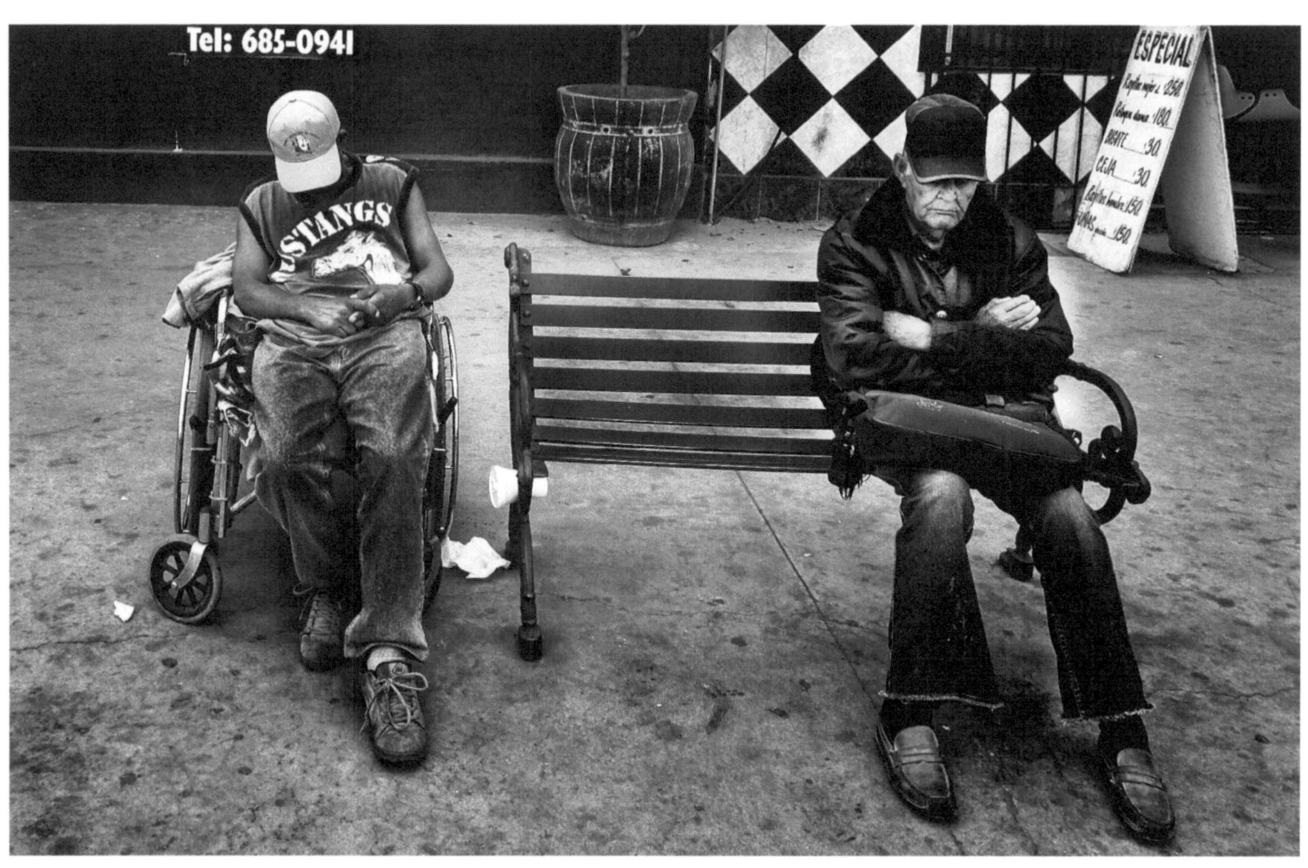
Tel: 685-0941
ESPECIAL
CEJA 30

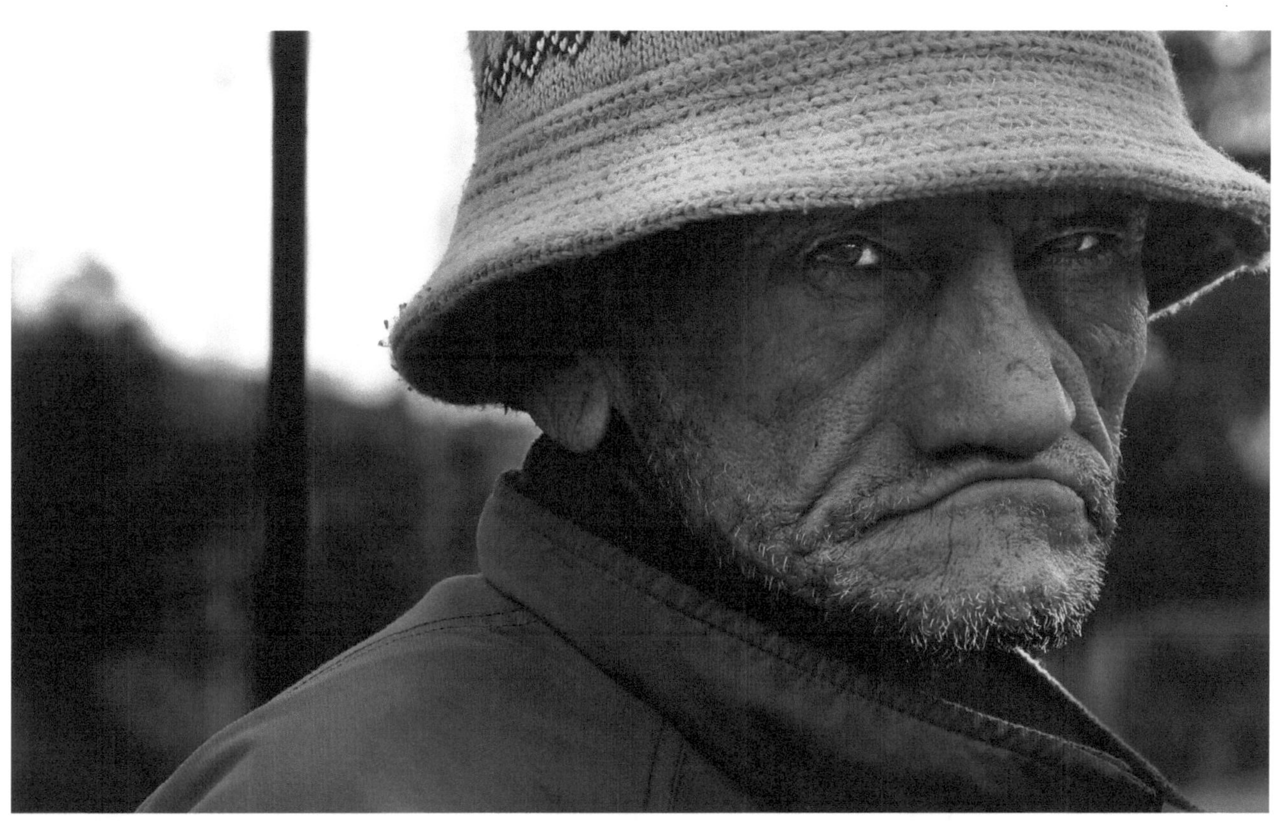

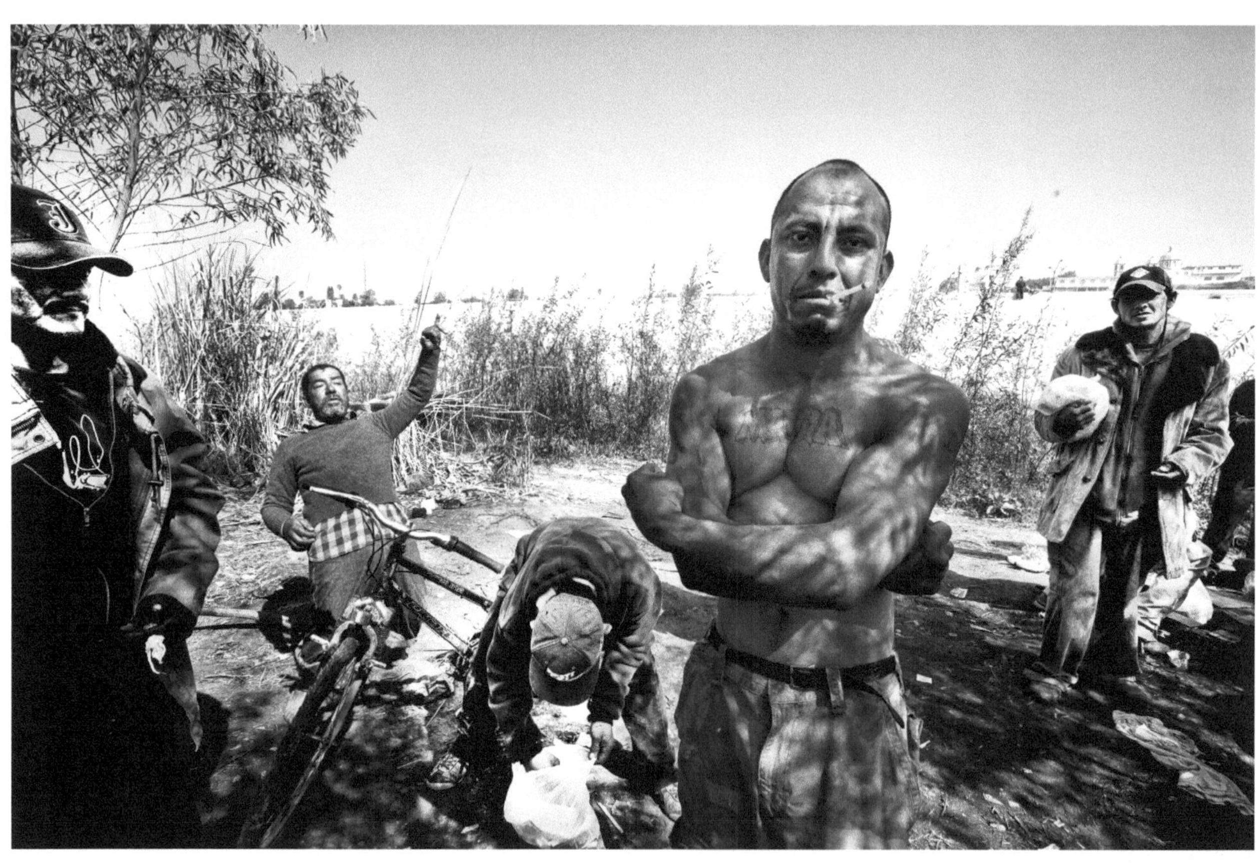

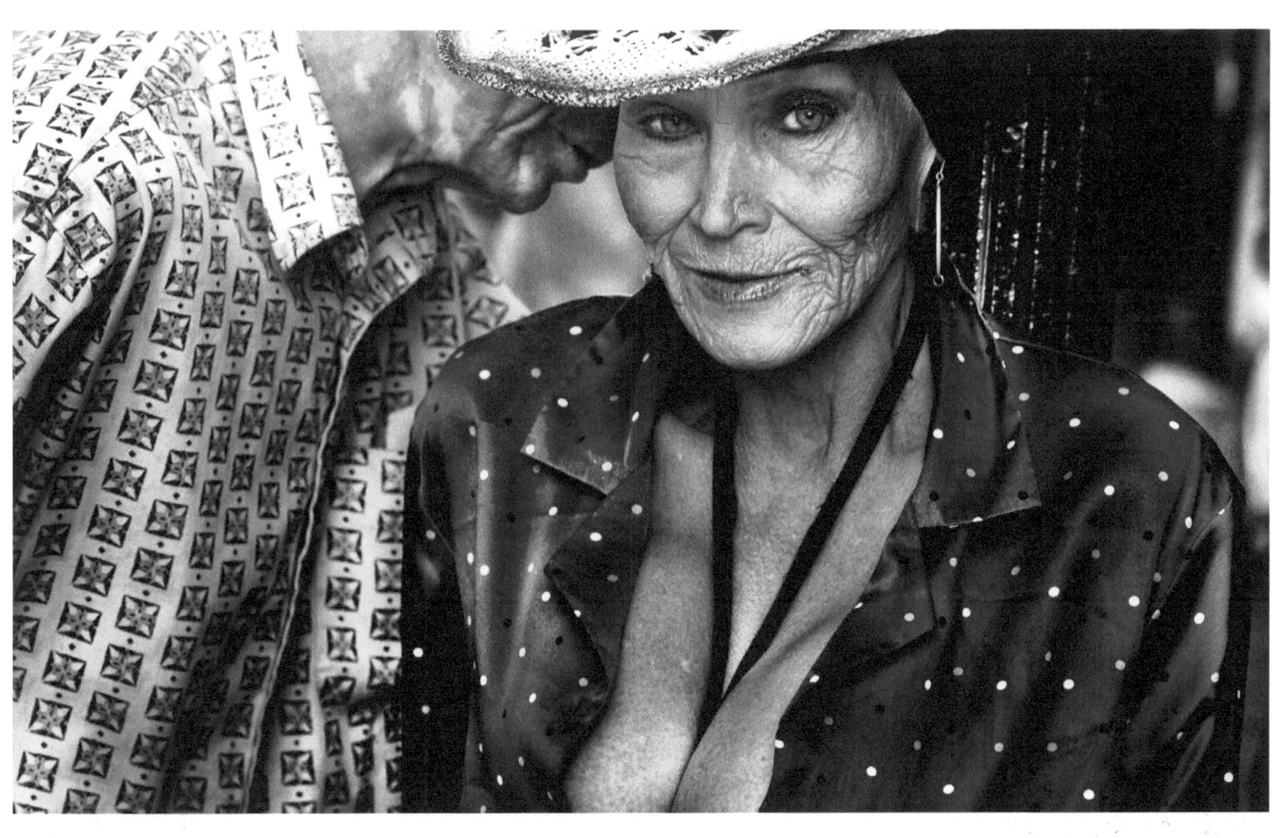

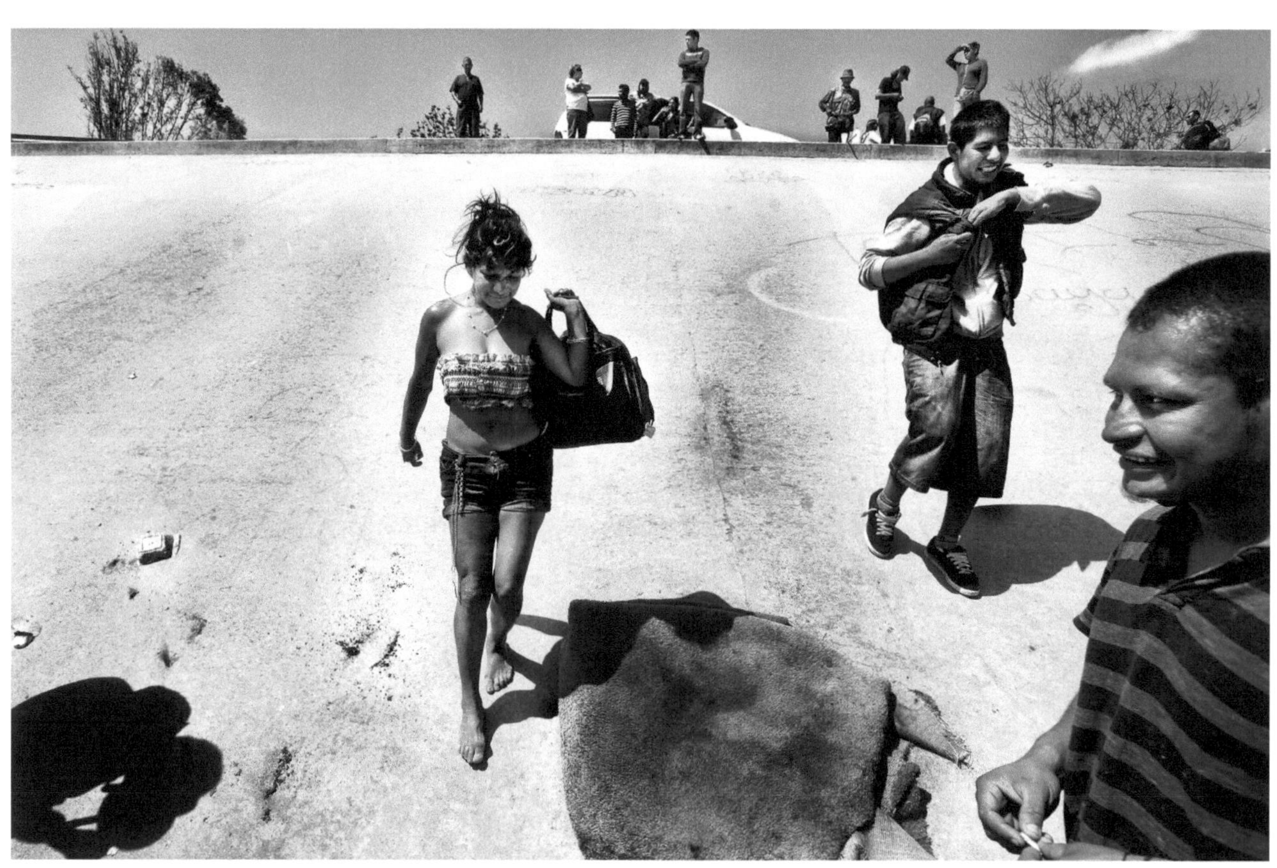

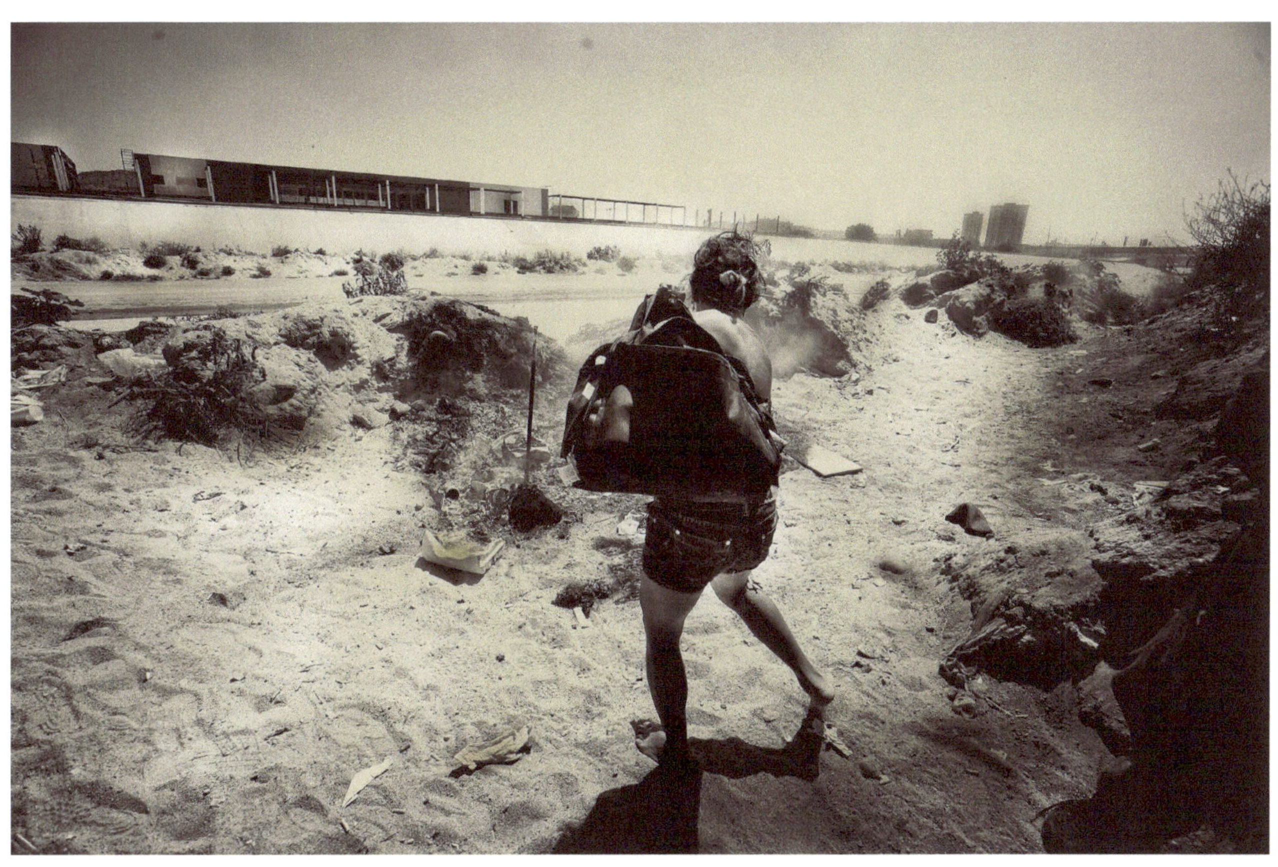

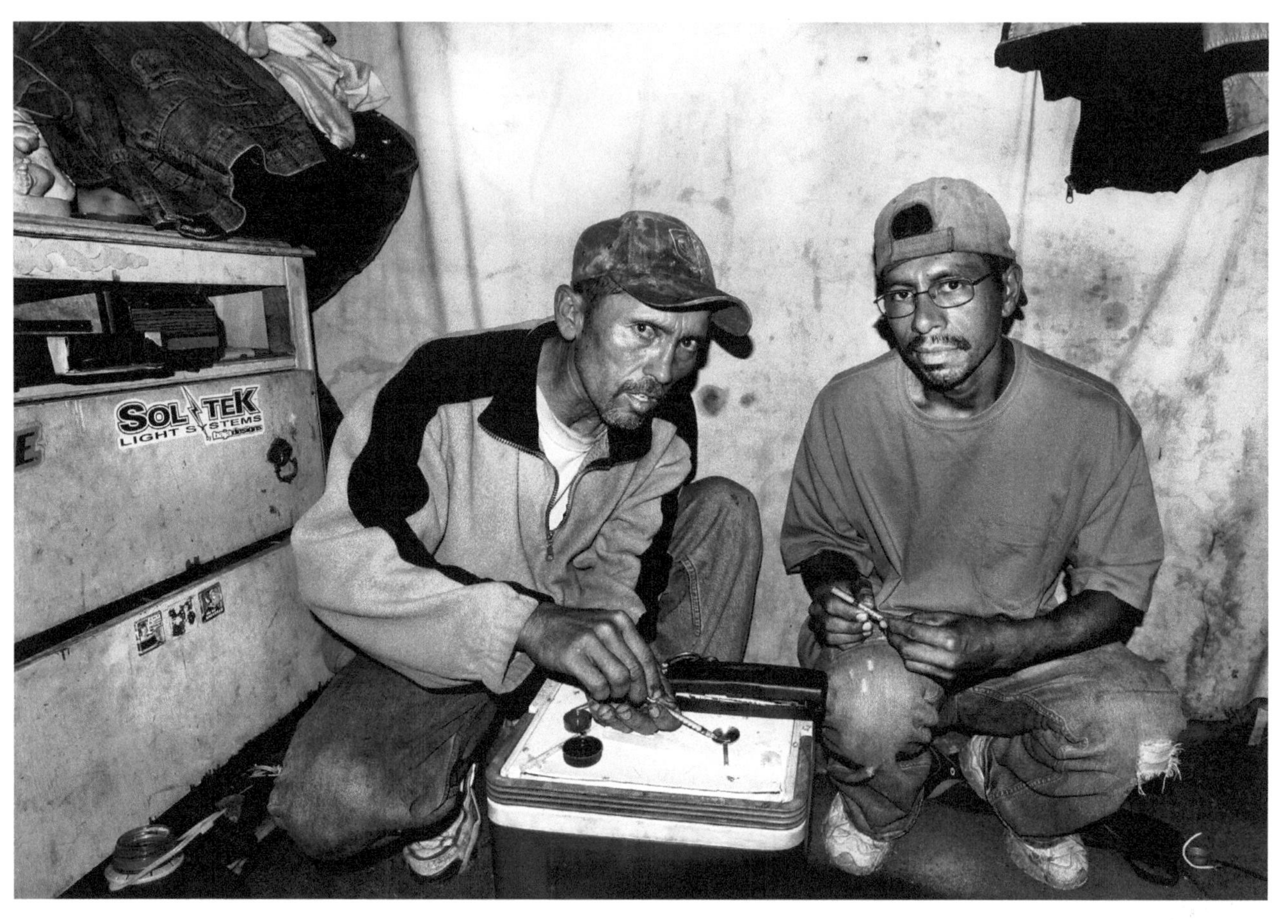
SOL TEK
LIGHT SYSTEMS

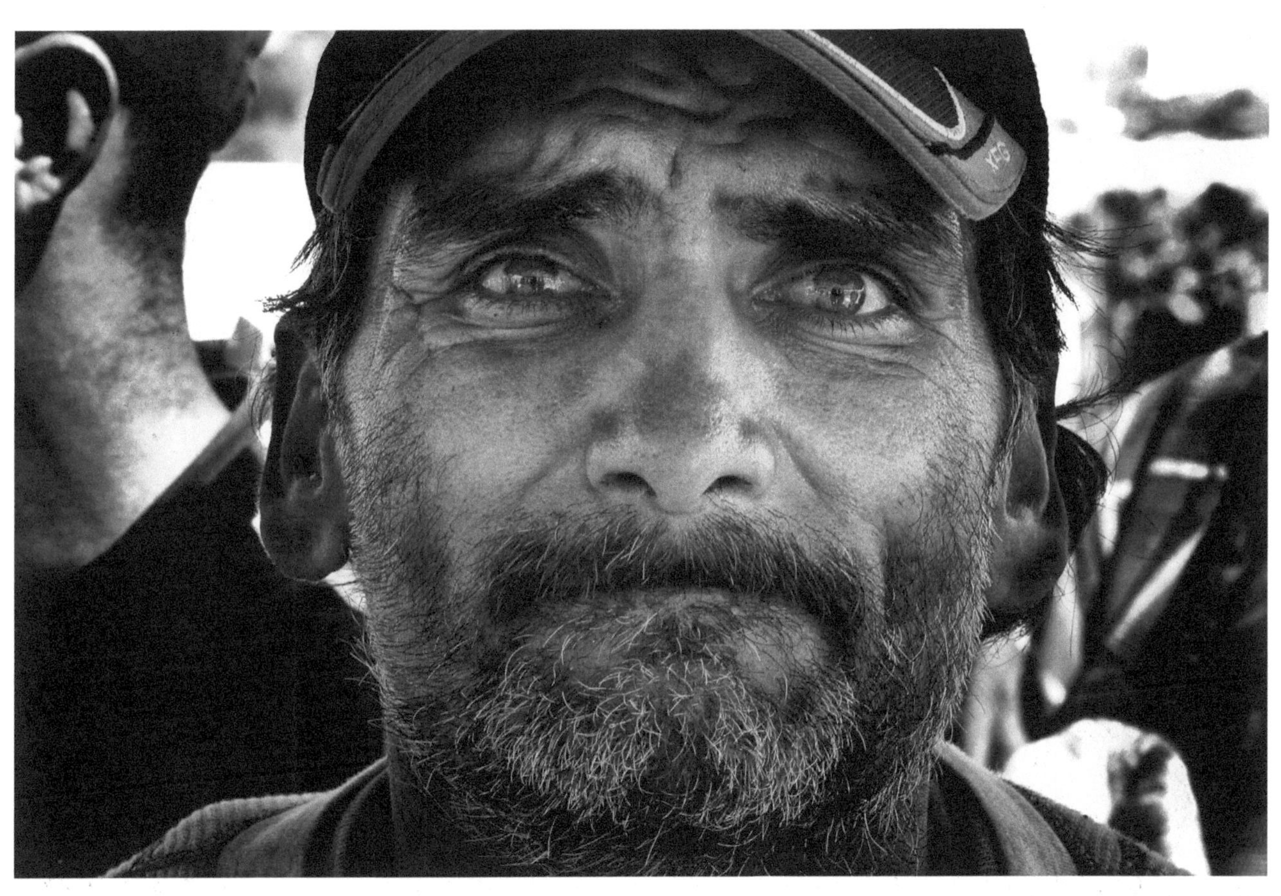

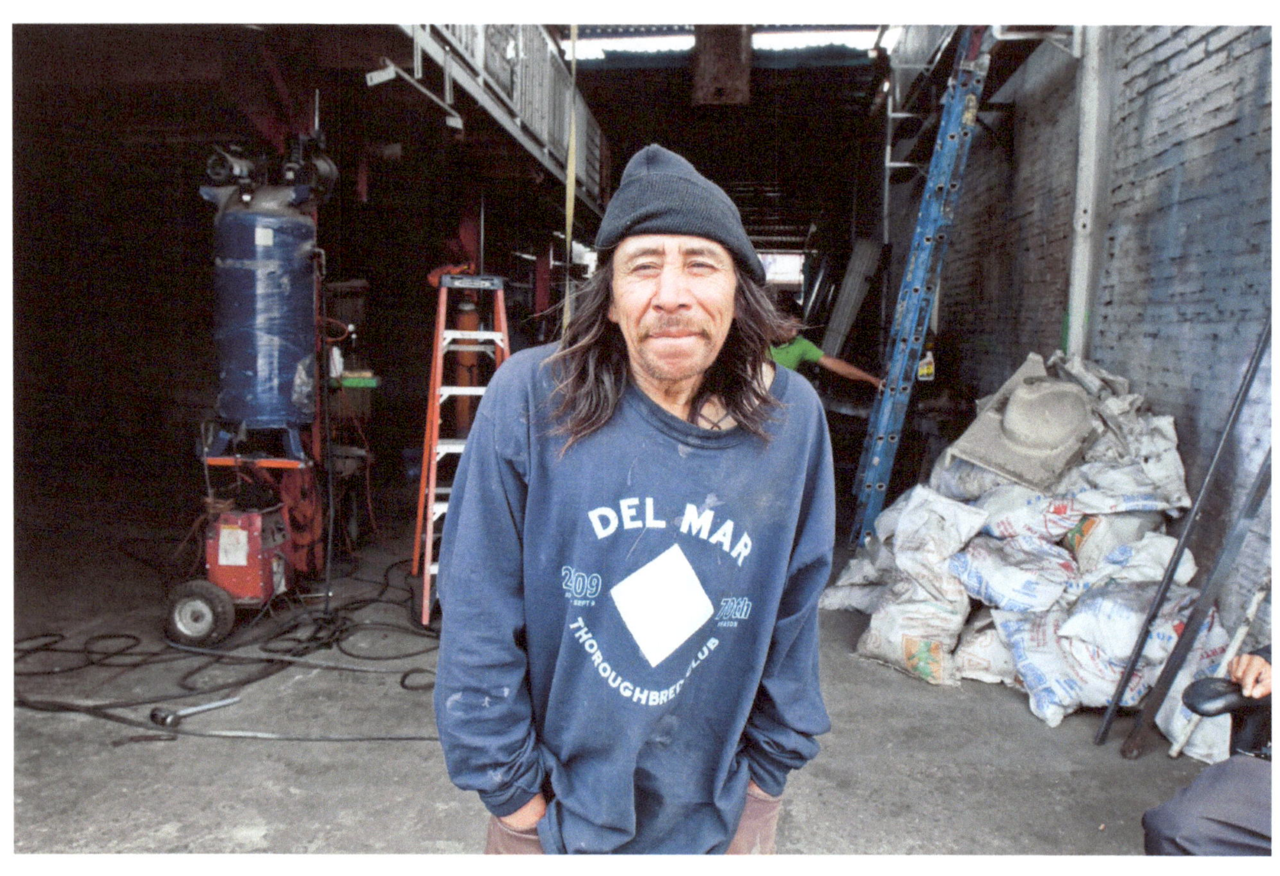
DEL MAR

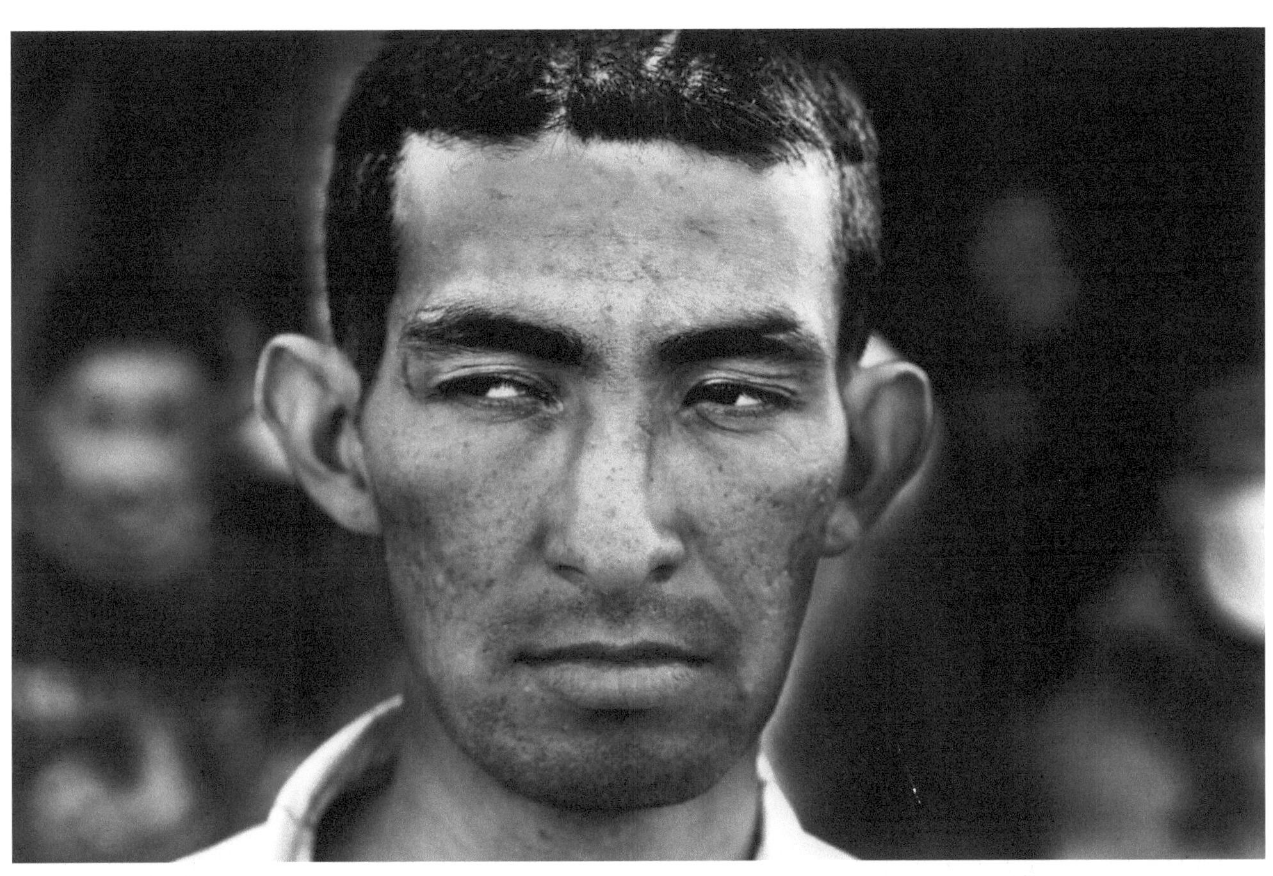

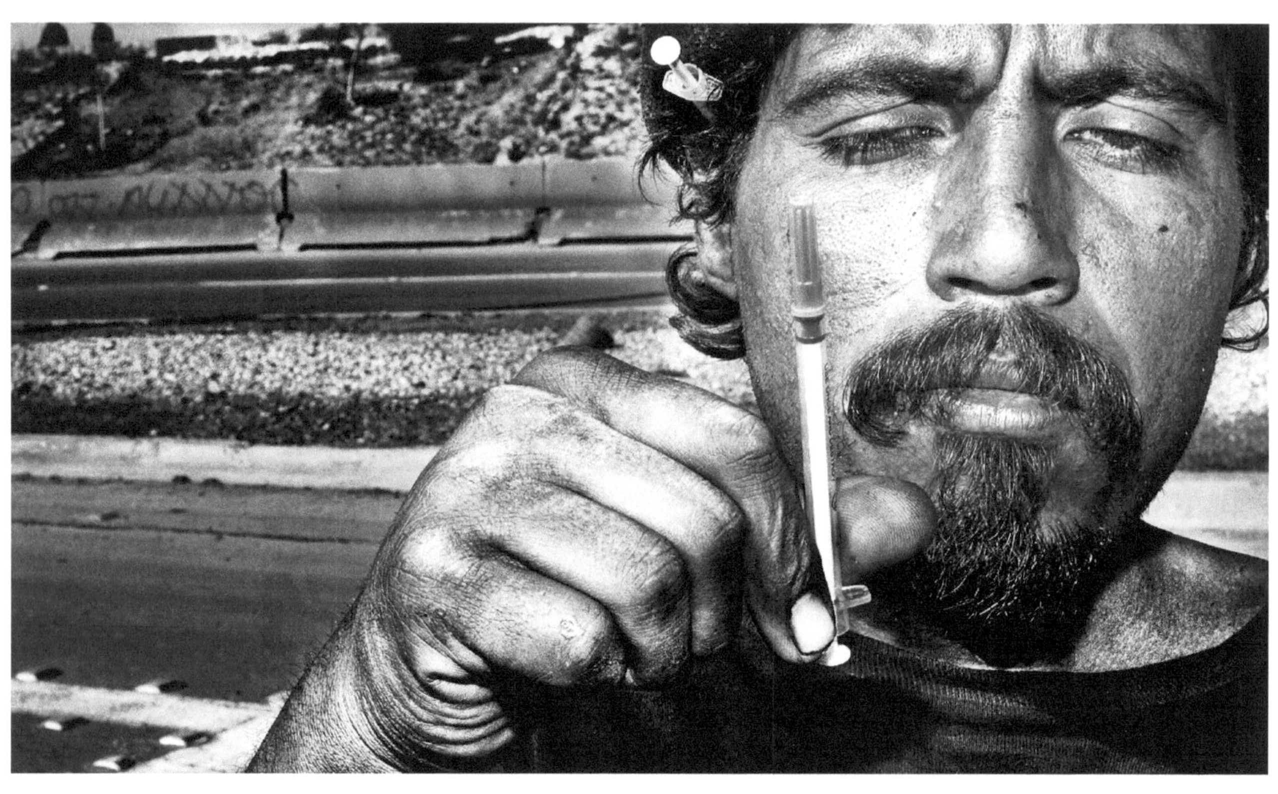

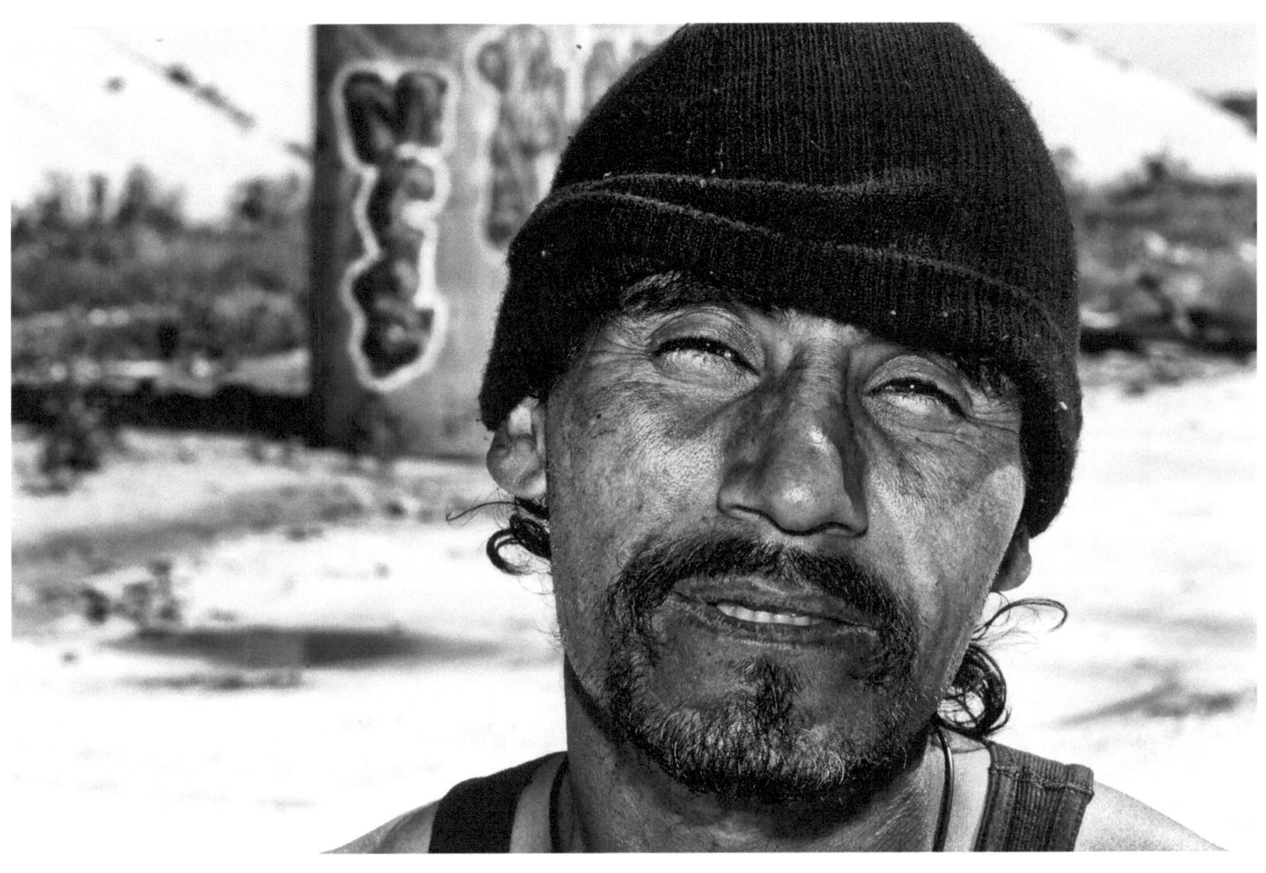

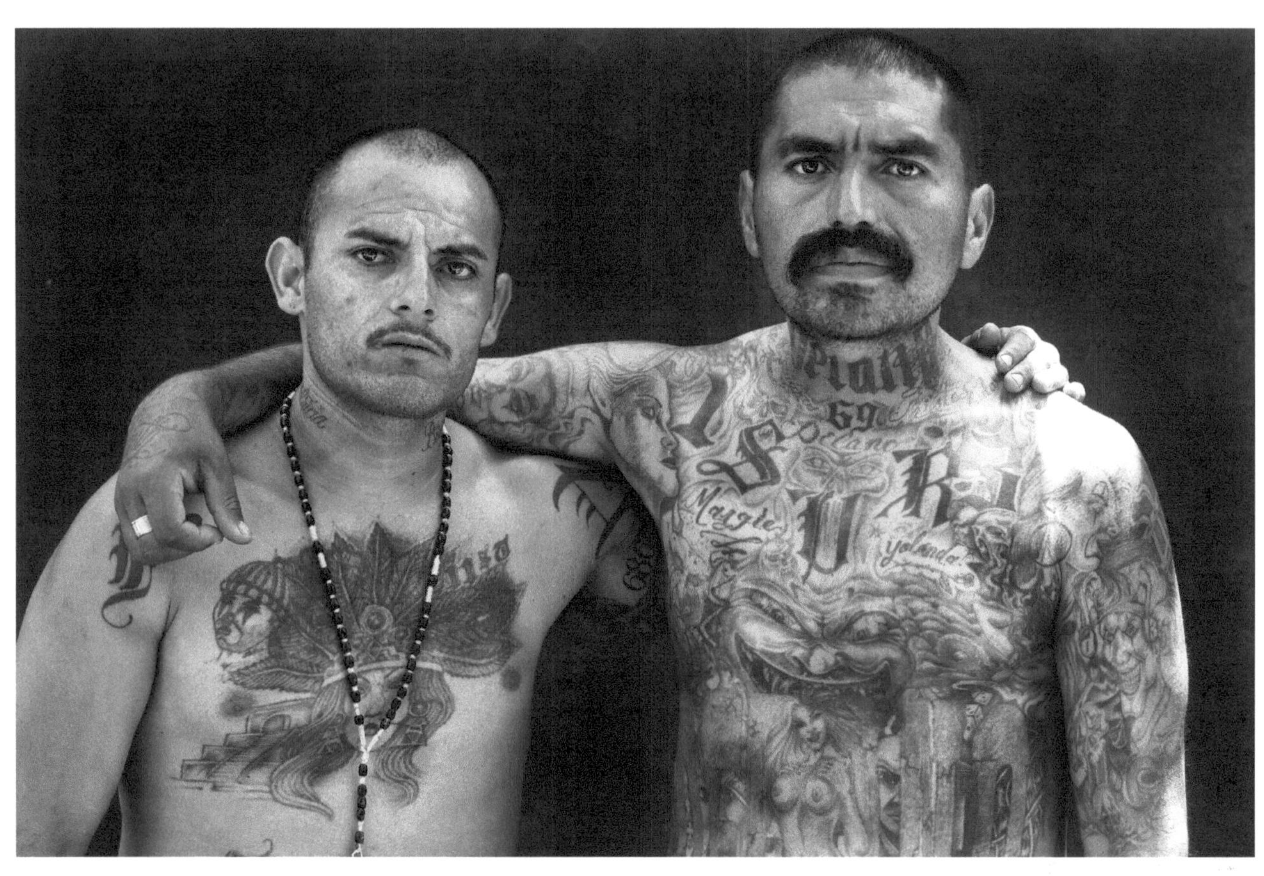

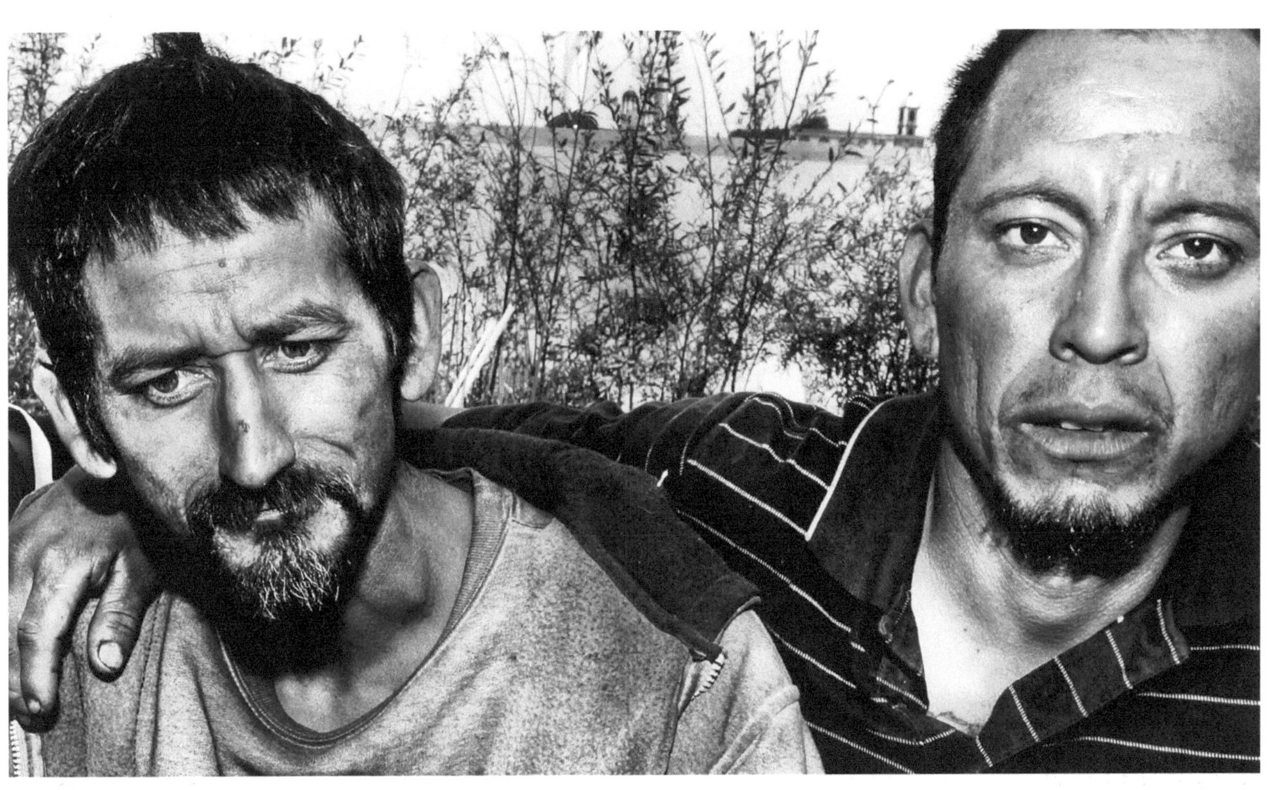

The United States of Hoodoo: Interview with Darius James

Ghazi Barakat

Darius James and I first met in the late nineties in NYC. We encountered each other again a couple of years later when we were both living in Berlin, and developed a friendship. He helped me write a bio for my musical project, Boy from Brazil, *and we collaborated on subcultural events in Berlin until he returned to the U.S. in 2007. After five years of sporadic correspondence, Darius came back to Germany in the summer of 2012 to present a documentary movie in which he stars called* The United States of Hoodoo. *The film premiered in Frankfurt and Berlin in late July, and I had the honor of playing a special Voodoo set at the after-party. Darius was kind enough to suggest to the editors of* Sensitive Skin *that I conduct the following interview—more honor, more death, more glory. We hung out at my Kreuzberg flat early this August and ran the voodoo down like we used to, only this time, a tape was running.*

—Ghazi Barakat

GHAZI: Making a film seems like a logical followup to *Negrophobia* and *That's Blaxploitation!*—they're both very cinematic books—*TB* even had the little flip-book movie in it! What's it like to be working in cinema?

DARIUS: I discovered that you need smart people to make a good film. It doesn't matter how much money you have. If you're all on the same page, relatively speaking, and focused, it can happen. I've always wanted to be involved in films, since I was a child. I started making eight-millimeter movies when I was a kid, and I continued making small films up to puberty. That changed when I discovered writing—you know, film requires a lot of money, equipment and people. Whereas you sit down with a pen and paper and you can write.

G: But making films is more of a communal experience.

D: Which is great, I want to continue with filmmaking.

G: With Oliver [Hardt, director and cowriter of *United States of Hoodoo*]? You have new ideas?

D: I'm working with someone now on a new project that concerns the darker aspects of Sammy Davis Junior's life.

G: Wasn't Sammy Davis a member of the Church of Satan?

D: Yes, which is the reason I got involved in the project.

G: I remember the parts with Sammy Davis in Linda Lovelace's book *Ordeal,* which was wonderful. How did the idea for *United States of Hoodoo* come about, since you cowrote the script and also appear in the movie?

D: The idea for a book started probably in 1985, maybe 1986.

G: What kind of book was this going to be?

D: I wanted to do a book on voodoo. Previously, I had been employed as a researcher for Michael O'Donoghue, the former *National Lampoon* and *Saturday Night Live* writer. I was working specifically on the *Easy Rider* sequel. It was called *Biker Heaven.* There was a sequence in the film that involved these bike-riding pagan witches. Part of my job was to get real information on witches. So I got involved with a group of witches from the Lower East Side and learned a number of spells, things like that, and different pseudo traditions of paganistic feminist witchcraft, okay? Through that experience, I became rather proficient in doing certain kinds of spells. What I didn't realize at the time was that the process of doing these spells always involved candle-gazing meditation. That is where the real power comes from—meditation. This internal psychic energy is what you're drawing from. This energy was never really something external. At a certain point, these witches got pissed at me and started throwing curses at the apartment I was living in. This was my first wizard war. At the end of this episode, I was on a train to New Haven and I ran into somebody from the New Haven occult scene. They told me that these people were pissed that I had a certain power object that was given to me by a former member of their coven. Basically, they said they didn't want black people involved in what they were doing. "We're Celts," they said. "We're Druids. We're white people and blah blah blah. What you need to do is get involved with voodoo."

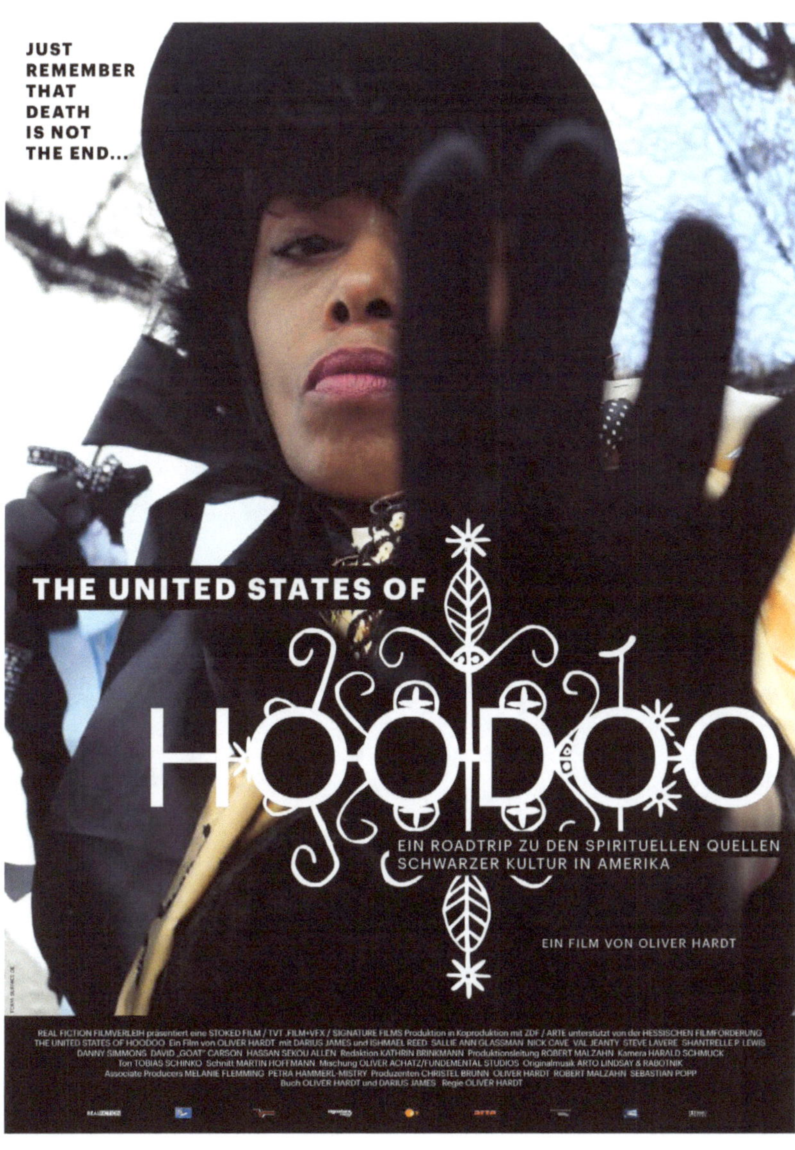

G: I remember you telling me, a few years ago, about the idea of a voodoo cookbook . . .

D: Well, I'm starting from the beginning. What eventually happened is that my friend Sally, whom I've been corresponding with for years—

G: Sally is in the movie?

D: Yes, the voodoo priestess in the film. We've known each other since high school. She was aware of me long before we met, because of her mother. Her mother was a drama teacher of mine and she use to come home and complain about me, so that's how Sally was aware of who I was. Let me see if I can speed this up a bit. Anyway, she was interested in the OTO, I hooked her up with the OTO, so she joined the OTO and eventually rose rather quickly through the ranks, where in fact she was the second in charge of this international order. If the caliph was out of the country for more than twenty-four hours, Sally was the official head of the order.

G: So we're still on the "white" black-magic side of the subject?

D: Yes. She eventually left the OTO for political

reasons. She devoted herself to the study of voodoo and became really adept. What people don't realize—because the question always comes up as to why this middle-aged Jewish white woman is talking about voodoo—is that she has lineage as far as spiritual study is concerned—like, who is your teacher? Who is your teacher's teacher? Who is their teacher? So there is a lineage, a line, like the students in kung fu movies. Sally is a direct linear descendant of Maya Deren, the dancer/filmmaker/author, who's known for her experimental films and this anthropological documentary called *Divine Horsemen,* as well as a book of the same title. Now, who was Maya Deren's teacher? That was Katherine Dunham. Katherine Dunham was a choreographer and anthropologist who is responsible for, among many other things, introducing authentic vodoun dance into Hollywood films. She is best known for *Cabin in the Sky.* She did the dance sequence at the end of the film *Stormy Weather,* the title song of which Lena Horne sang. Now, the thing with Katherine Dunham is, she trained, or so-called "initiated," a number of important black American choreographers into the nature of vodoun dance. Alvin Ailey, Geoffrey Holder, Lena Horne, all of whom were once members of her dance company. Eartha Kitt, these people, you know. Except, here, vodoun dance is presented as art, a religious experience behind the mask of art. Whereas in more forbidden times, during the times of slavery, voodoo was masked by Catholicism, saints, things like that, and nowadays voodoo wears the mask of art. Art is where you can project vodoun energies, but it's known by a different name. I think what I should do now is define what voodoo is. Voodoo is a religion, it's a religion that's danced, that's transmitted through music, e.g., drum rhythms and song. The combination puts one in a trance state where the ego is lost and is replaced by a feeling of ecstasy, a feeling of the divine, a feeling of God.

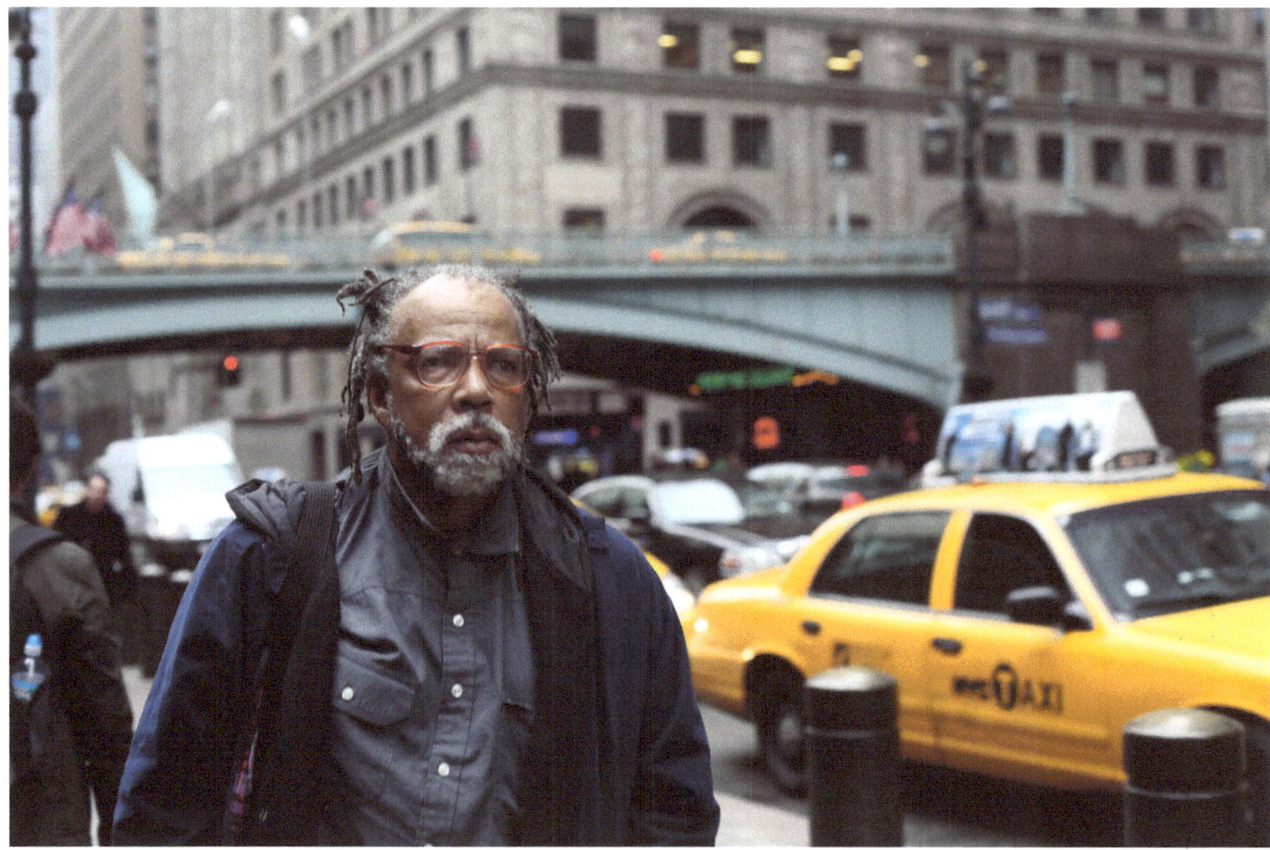

G: I always thought that voodoo was also the beginning of psychoanalysis through psychodrama, by living out certain taboos, by doing the things you can't really do in normal society. That you can live out all these energies that are obviously in us—Greek mythology for me has a similar function. It's more than just religion, it's resolving inner conflicts in the community and with yourself. In Haitian voodoo, you get possessed by a spirit of the opposite sex, like the very feminine Erzulie, which might be helpful to overcome homophobia, but maybe that came from the pirates, maybe it's different in Benin.

D: I don't know about Benin. I'm trying to talk about how voodoo has manifested in American culture. Obviously, there are many miles between Africans and African-Americans. African-Americans aren't simply African-Americans, they are many things. I had the idea for this project for years. I was stopped from doing it for various reasons. In Berlin, I found myself in a position where I could finally work on it. So I wrote a proposal of about forty pages for a book. I gave it to my then so-called agents to shop around. They kept coming back with rejections from all the major New York publishing houses. What my agents were telling me was, one, the editors wanted me to take an academic approach, which I refused to do, because there are too many academic books on the subject and I think it should be approached from a personal, exploratory point of view. What does it feel like, the voodoo experience, you know? And, two, they all claimed they didn't understand what I wanted to do. When that happened, I sent the first few pages of the proposal to Oliver Hardt, whom I had worked with previously on a documentary called *Black Deutschland.* This was a film about blacks in Germany. I sent it to him because English was his second language, and if he didn't understand what I wanted to do, that meant there was something wrong with my writing. I was communicating ineffectively. If he came back and said he understood, then there was something fucked up with the editors who rejected the project. So he came back to me and said he understood the project perfectly and in fact he would like to make a film based on what I had presented. And from there, he spent three years raising the money from a film company he's a part of in Frankfurt, and they managed to get some money from Arte.

G: So it was a lucky accident. You just wanted his opinion and he said, "I'll do it!"

D: Yeah.

G: *The United States of Hoodoo* is a very personal road movie revolving around your history and cultural interests. I wanted to know your personal standpoint towards cinema as a writer and also under which criteria you chose the characters involved. You've talked about Sally already, and it seems you had her in mind from the beginning, but there are also the other quite interesting characters.

D: I did a lot of studying and talked to a lot of people from the beginning. I started this in 2000. I corresponded with a number of people that I wanted to include in this project. Obviously, many of them didn't even get to the interview stage. Lots of people were either people that I knew previously, who had a feeling for the subject I wanted to talk about. Some of them I met on the road, some of them were people that Oliver had discovered. So basically, we put these people together.

G: How did you discover Val, the Haitian girl who lives in New York and makes this amazing modern electronic voodoo jazz?

D: She was one of the people whom Oliver had found. He had gone to an exhibition at the Caribbean Cultural Center, and he saw a videotape and thought she might be interesting. I saw a video clip and listened to her music, and I thought why not, we can talk with her. However, when we actually shot, it was the first time I had met her, and I could tell she was the real thing. Because of her music, yes, but [also because], when we entered into her space, she was totally serious. Not because of the altars and the various power objects within—it was just the vibe she gave off, the vibe in the apartment, and we hit it off like that. It was natural. We met Hassan on the day we shot in Sally's temple. In the film, you see him coming in on a bicycle, dressed in white, and he smiles at camera. That's the first time we'd ever seen him. Because he was one of the few black faces in a sea of white people, Oliver thought it might be a good idea to speak with him.

G: That's the piano player who explains the rhythms? What's his full name?

D: Hassan Sekou Allen. There's also Joe Marini, whom I met New Year's Eve 2006. I was stumbling out of a bar in Manhattan and he, just, out of the blue, said, "You have Indian blood, don't you?" And I said, "Yeah!" And he said, "I could tell," and went into this whole spirit-reading thing.

G: Who is he in the movie?

D: He appears briefly while we're talking with Danny Simmons in his apartment in Brooklyn with all the masks. He's the Palo Mayombe priest. He was really interesting.

G: They both seemed to be. I liked their attitude, anthropological on one side, but also very human. Very open, and a nice vibe toward the whole subject.

D: I mean, that was Joe's life. He comes from a family of Santeros, and he went to what some might consider the "darker side" of Santeria.

G: Is there an even darker side of Santeria? I thought Santeria is already on the dark side.

D: Well, there are people within the religion who deal specifically with demons, and that was his speciality.

G: So he's an exorcist?

D: Yeah, he wrestles with demons, communicates with them. I mean, these are people who literally talk with spirits. You look at them and they're just off, like, babbling. I mean, Sally's papa, Edgar, whom we didn't really explore in the film—he's mentioned, we acknowledge him in the film. When I first met him a few years before, the guy would just sit in a garden, you know, talk to the trees, various spirits, things like that. I mean, he was out! Sally acted as an interpreter between us, and we just had this wild conversation, 'cause I don't speak French Creole, French Haitian Creole, or any kind of French.

G: She's Creole?

D: No, she's a Russian-American Jew.

G: Because you said *papa,* I thought it was her father. You meant *hougan?*

D: Yeah, the papa. They are seen as family, and we're talking lineage, right? Because most people who are raised in those traditions are raised in it through their family.

G: The three main facets of the feature are art, music and cuisine. Is there a red line going through your journey in regard to those?

D: Yes, there was a red line: they were connections I had already made. In terms of cooking, drawing from different cuisines to create this unique thing. You know, if you look at old witchcraft books from the seventies that have spells in them, [they] look like cookbooks.

G: Well, yeah, they're recipes.

D: So I think of food the same way.

G: What were you looking for during this journey? Did you find it?

D: I can answer that question, but it sounds pretentious. What I was looking for in the film is what I'm looking for in my own life. For spiritual wholeness, "enlightenment." All things are interrelated, they converge into "the one," if we are all one. Reality is an illusion, and the point of a lot of spiritual practice is to cut through the bullshit that makes up most of our "reality" and bring us to a true sense of the divine. That's what I want. That's what I'm looking for.

G: So it's a desire?

D: Yeah. So did I find that through the experience of the film? I got closer to it. I discovered a lot of interesting things that I need to pursue further. I think the most important person I met on the film—for me—was Val, the electronic drummer.

G: Yeah, she was fascinating. For me, she almost didn't get enough coverage. The film starts with her and I was like, okay, now we're talking, and then she didn't reappear. She seemed to be more difficult to integrate, and she coming from a completely different angle.

D: Actually it was through my adherence with her,

'cause originally I was going to do the whole initiation trip with Sally and becoming an official devotee of voodoo. Whereas I discovered through Val that I didn't need to do that, I was already a member of the family—a family of loas, the Gede family.

G: Did you find something that you *weren't* looking for? Any surprises, in either a good or a bad way?

D: No, I think we were pretty blessed. I think the surprises are gonna happen now. When I started this whole thing in 2000, I was told that I was going to be tested a lot. By the orishas, the loas, the African powers.

G: You mean the laws. *Loa* is French patois for the word *loi*, which means "the law."

D: That's interesting. I mean, what I realized with Val is that her music is a purely spiritual thing. It's a spiritual system that she was working with.

G: What was it like traveling in the South?

D: What I didn't really expect was that the South itself was time-locked back, like, 50, 60 years.

G: You didn't know that?

D: No, because I had never been to the South.

G: When I was living in New York, I was always thinking, this is not America. Let's move down south and look for the real America where the blues and rock & roll come from. But the fact that they're backwards gives it some wholesomeness—no-change is reassuring, it's not torn by modern technology. When Robert Johnson comes up in the movie, he seems to

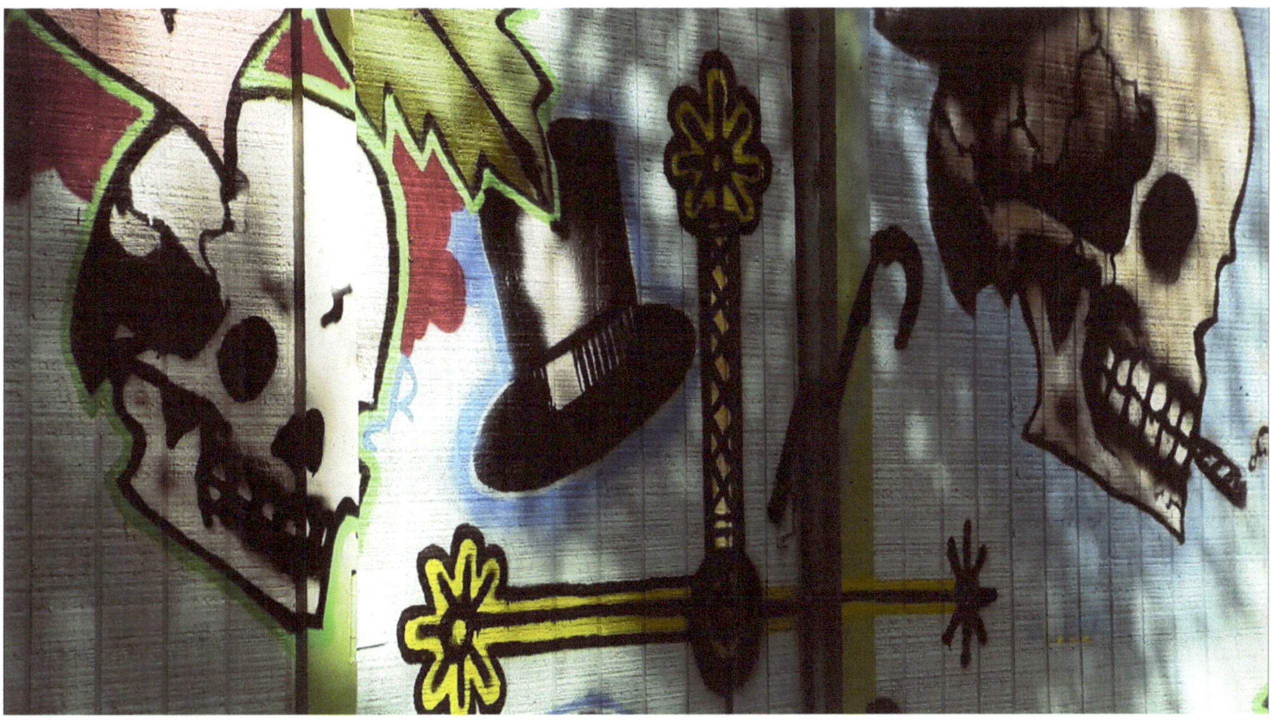

be very much alive in people's heads, although there is probably barely anyone still alive who knew him.

D: There was one person who apparently knew Robert Johnson, but he unfortunately didn't make it to the blues fest in Greenwoods Park.

G: But you found out how he actually died?

D: I was expecting to go to the actual crossroads where Robert Johnson made his so-called deal with the devil. That didn't happen. What did happen was that I found myself on the highway where Emmett Till was picked up and murdered.

G: Who's Emmett Till?

D: Emmett Till was a black teenager from Chicago

who was visiting relatives in Mississippi. He went into a shop and he whistled at a white girl. She was offended and complained, and some people in town got pissed and lynched him. He was, like, 14,15,16 years old. It's the first incident where white people involved in a lynching were actually prosecuted. They were taken to trial. I mean, they got off. That was sort of an early trauma for me.

G: So you didn't expect it, because you thought you were so far away from all this?

D: Yeah. One would think that the country had evolved, and then you realize it gets more and more retarded every day.

G: Well, that's idiocracy. So, did you learn how Robert Johnson died?

D: We were there during the Robert Johnson centennial, which seemed pretty ridiculous, because the centennial [celebration] and this exhibition were in a cotton museum, and Robert Johnson apparently spent his entire life avoiding the cotton fields. So you have all these weird white people celebrating Robert Johnson. The same people who would have shot him if they caught him outside of the cotton field. There were all these weird contradictions, like how far they had gotten. I got into some stupid discussion about who owns Robert Johnson. I kept wanting to make these nasty comments about the Rolling Stones, which I'm glad I didn't, as a result of reading Keith Richards's autobiography. What he says is true: that the Stones were probably single-handedly responsible for reintroducing the blues back to America.

. . . you have all these weird white people celebrating Robert Johnson. The same people who would have shot him if they caught him outside of the cotton field.

G: So what's the story of his demise?

D: I discovered, as a result of all the activities around the centennial, that the story that Robert Johnson told about himself, as far as selling his soul to the devil, was like early heavy-metal PR.

G: He was a blasphemer.

D: It wasn't that he was a blasphemer. His audience were sharecroppers and cotton-field workers. They were basically superstitious Christians.

G: But he did sing, "If I had possession over Judgment Day, Lord, the little woman I'm loving wouldn't have no right to pray." Let's say he was against organized religion.

D: Okay, that's fair, but I'm just saying that his rebellion against black Christian conservatism, which seemed to be prominent in his family—that's the thing I wasn't expecting! His great-great-grandson was there speaking at this church, which is also the churchyard where Robert is buried. He comes to speak, at the last minute—it was supposed to be a day to celebrate the life of R.J. because it's his birthday, which also happened to fall on Mother's Day. So what we get is this fat, greasy preacher who comes out and tells us that he is R.J.'s great-grandson, and he proceeds to spew the most repellent homophobic right-wing garbage I've ever heard in my life. What I found particularly offensive was when he went into the whole R.J. thing of selling his soul to the devil. *Mimics Richard Pryor.* "How can my black uncle, grandfather or whatever the fuck he was, sell his soul to the devil? His soul does not belong to him, it belongs to God! How can you trade with the devil something that belongs to God?" That was particularly repellent, to see how the church of the poor had been taken over by corrupt right-wing Christian fundamentalists.

G: So, did Robert Johnson get poisoned?

D: You know, these are great stories, great myths that add to the legend. I was sitting with a bunch of Robert Johnson scholars at a blues bar early in the morning. One of the things that seemed to be repeating itself was that Robert Johnson died as a result of drinking poisoned moonshine. The entire batch that had come into the honky-tonk for that weekend was bad, and the reason he died is because the audience he was playing to—again, sharecroppers, people who work in cotton fields—had to get up and go to work on Monday. He started on Saturday, played his gig, they went home, they were sick on Sunday, but apparently were well enough to go to work on Monday. Robert Johnson, who didn't spend a lot of time picking cotton in the cotton field, stayed at the honky-tonk and continued to drink this bad moonshine, got sick, and died.

G: At one point in the film, there is a discussion about how much Afro-Americans are willing to identify with their cultural and religious African roots. On a recent trip to Burkina Faso, I noticed that Africans are still mainly animistic, and that Wahhabite Muslim and Christian Baptist missionaries have a hard time persuading people to convert to monotheism. They usually resort to materialistic means, since poverty is the major issue on that continent. Many Afro-Americans, on the other hand, have embraced monotheism, be it through organizations like the Nation of Islam or traditional Christianity. Can you elaborate a bit on this?

D: In New York, and in other urban centers, you'll find African Americans—or black Americans, which I prefer—who will identify with genuine animistic, Afro-esoterics, but those numbers are smaller than the great, unwashed majority, who are largely concerned with the details of survival, not necessarily breaking taboos. There was a large majority of blacks in California who were opposed to gay marriage, which revealed this really mean right-wing reactionary streak in the black church right now, which wasn't always true—Martin Luther King came from liberation theology.

G: A key moment in the movie is when you talk about how the Africans and the Native Americans were able to assimilate one another, since there were so many cultural similarities between the two. This fusion happened in places like New Orleans, and an island like Haiti, and in South America, where slaves and natives were outcasts and in large numbers. Vodoun has survived and actually evolved into a gumbo of cultural misfits. This is most obvious in the carnival parades of all these places, but then, in the film there is a voodoo ceremony where most people involved are white women.

D: Well, Sally's temple has always occupied a rather controversial place because of that. There are vodoun cults in the United States who recognize voodoo as a way of getting back to roots and see Sally as polluting the religion, that it is not something that belongs to her, which, clearly—it's God we're talking about here. God belongs to everybody, the divine belongs to everybody. The invisible is invisible for a reason.

G: So her cult is progressive and some are regressive, although most non-African voodoo cults evolved or became mutations as a political necessity.

D: It becomes an identity, but the whole point of voodoo is to lose your identity in the face of the divine.

G: Besides the spiritual aspect, is there a political aspect to voodoo?

D: Absolutely. The reason why voodoo has a bad reputation is because a bunch of black people kicked some white people off an island, you know, threw off the shackles of slavery, and they're still pissed.

FIND OUT MORE ABOUT *THE UNITED STATES OF HOODOO,* AND SEE A TRAILER, AT THE OFFICIAL WEBSITE:

http://hoodoo.stokedfilm.com/

New Bedford Real Estate

Amman Sabet

Usually, I tell people I'm from around Boston, but I'm not even from there. I grew up just outside New Bedford. It's a port city on the South Shore that used to be big on whaling. You got lots of ugly Portuguese there. I live and work in L.A. now and when I tell my coworkers where I'm from, the most I ever get is:

"So is that near Cape Cod?"

"Yeah," I'll say.

"I went to Martha's Vineyard when I was a kid," they might say.

"Oh yeah?" I'd say.

Yeah. Nobody from New Bedford ever left to go live somewhere else where people actually use their brains. Not my parents or my friends or anybody else. They're all just a bunch of brain-zombies there. Nothing ever happened in New Bedford other than graduation or someone having a kid.

Me and some guys from high school used to race cars to cut the boredom. We'd buy these shitbox clunkers listed in Autotrader and install all kinds of aftermarket parts to make them roll faster. On a given Sunday, there'd be like three or four of us drinking beers in a garage, tuning these beasts. When a part was incompatible we'd work a miracle just to keep them running. Then the sun would set and we'd burn up the state roads like a bunch of retards.

I was there the night Anthony DiGinnaro flipped his Nissan Skyline. I was racing him. He was banking hard, trying to keep ahead of my Mark II but he kept fishtailing 'cause his power train was weird and his ABS wasn't set up. Grinding out this one sharp turn near the Fall River exit, he hit a hole in the road and, boom, popped his front left tire. Skyline lost traction, hit the barrier going like sixty or something and flipped over it. Crunch. Dude went through the windshield and hit a tree.

All my friends went to the funeral, but I didn't go. Nobody knew it was me he was racing, but showing up just didn't feel right.

I started having these nightmares about keeping Anthony's engine in my dad's basement, like I'd lifted it out of his wrecked Skyline somehow. We'd be eating dinner but that engine would be on a cinder block downstairs running hot. I'd come down 'cause of the noise and there it was, pistons firing redder and redder and smoking up the space. I'd wake up screaming.

"It's just stress," My dad said. "Your mother used to be like that."

I cracked and told him about the race. We got into a fight about the whole thing.

"You oughta be ashamed," he said. "What if you hit someone?"

Euthanasia by car? No different than the movies, when people drive into a big crowd of zombies. Kinda like bowling. I threw it back in his face. I don't know why. Maybe I was disappointed at how he had no crazy story of his own to absolve me with. Something about how, back in the day, he and Uncle Beamish used to put their toes right up to the edge, too. He didn't have any stories like that. I kind of felt like I had outgrown him.

So I sold my Mark II and bought a plane ticket with the money, thinking I'd cut out and see California. I got on the plane with just a duffel bag. I never got into acting or producing, but I did end up with a few office gigs. My dad thought I was only gonna be gone for a little while, but I never came back until now.

I didn't make a big deal about it at first. I figured I wanted a few days just to be by myself. Mirna knows I came back, though. She was my dad's neighbor. She saw me fiddling with the keys at the front door after getting out of the cab.

"You want me to keep it a secret?" she says with a

nasal sort of New England accent that comes from the top of the throat.

"Yeah."

"OK. I can't tell nobody you're back? What about Lizette? Remember her? We work together at Davy's Locker now."

I remember her. "Yeah, all right."

"You gonna sell your dad's house?"

"That's what I'm back for," I say. Key is in the door.

"Huh. Well, if you want, my cousin can come clean it for ya."

"Maybe next week. See you tomorrow?"

"Yeah," Mirna says from her front steps. She surveys her lawn from under her aluminum awning like she'd just noticed how dark it was outside. "Lemme know if you need something, 'kay?"

#

My dad's house is an old Georgian colonial. Unlike the rest of the houses on the street, his is set back away from the curb. The driveway goes right down the middle of the lawn, splitting it into two patches of grass you can't really do much of nothing with. I never played football or catch growing up because Dad's truck would be in the way.

The driveway goes right down the middle of the lawn, splitting it into two patches of grass you can't really do much of nothing with. I never played football or catch growing up because Dad's truck would be in the way.

The entire right side of the house is covered by a big bush. It's such a big bastard of a bush that I think everyone in the family stopped using that side of the house, you know? The basement windows haven't even been cleaned in years 'cause no one can get to them.

The stairs creak, echoing in the stairwell when I come up to my old room. Uncle Beamish already came and took away most of Dad's furniture, but there's still a mattress and frame done up sort of nice and I remember when my dad used my room for storage after I moved out.

The headlights from passing cars strafe across the ceiling and wall, cut into squares by the windowsill. I hear a faint hum and I think at first that it's a fog horn passing through the harbor, but then I realize that my phone is vibrating inside my roller bag. I ignore it. Now that none of our stuff is in the house anymore I see how the rooms were just a bunch of lines and planes that organized all that stuff into squares.

An hour later, I wake up to the sound of someone banging on the front door.

"Jimaaay!" I hear from outside.

My shirttails hiked themselves out of my pants in my sleep. I walk over to the window and look down.

"Jim, you in there?"

A car in the driveway has its headlights on, flooding the bottom floor windows. It's Vinnie. His breath is steaming in the headlights. Even in his Bruins jacket, I can tell he gained weight. I shuffle downstairs in the dark to meet him.

"Oh shit, what's up?" he says and slaps my hand. The slap lingers and turns into a handshake, then leans into a back-pat, creaking the screen door out of the way.

"Hey, you wanna come in?"

Vin looks over my shoulder at the emptiness of the house. "Nah, come out real quick. Mirna told Lizette you were back. Come get beers."

"I can't, man. I gotta be up—"

"It's Saturday. What do you got tomorrow?"

I think about lying to him. I don't actually have to meet the real estate lady until Monday.

Vin is one of my closest friends and I haven't seen him in three years. Back in high school, he used to be really into Jiu-Jitsu. When I asked his sister Lizette out, he chaperoned us around, since he was the only one with a car. He'd put me in arm locks and joke about clobbering me for dating his sister.

After two weeks, Lizette and I broke up, but he and I kept hanging out. We'd smoke weed out by the Lloyd Center marshlands and karate-kick old wooden palates apart.

Vin is driving. "What happened to your old car?" I ask.

"The Camaro? Sold it. Thing barely turned over anymore. I traded it for a boat."

"You got a whole boat for that?"

"Nah," he shakes his head. "Like a little dinghy boat. I bought this one from the dealership on Route 6. Warranty's still on it, so I'm gonna wait on parts."

I punch in the lighter and light a Parliament. Then I crack the window, flick the ash and pinch a thread of tobacco off my tongue with my pinky and thumb. The movement makes me think of all the streets I had bombed down in Vin's old Camaro, going nowhere.

"So what's it been, like, a million years?" he says, glancing from the road over to me. Then he grabs my sleeve and shakes me a little to emphasize his excitement and the car swerves.

"Where are we going?" I ask.

"My mom's. I've got something to give you and she wants to say hi."

"Hows your sister?" I ask. "We stopping by Davy's Locker tonight?"

"You're gonna start with that shit already?" Vin

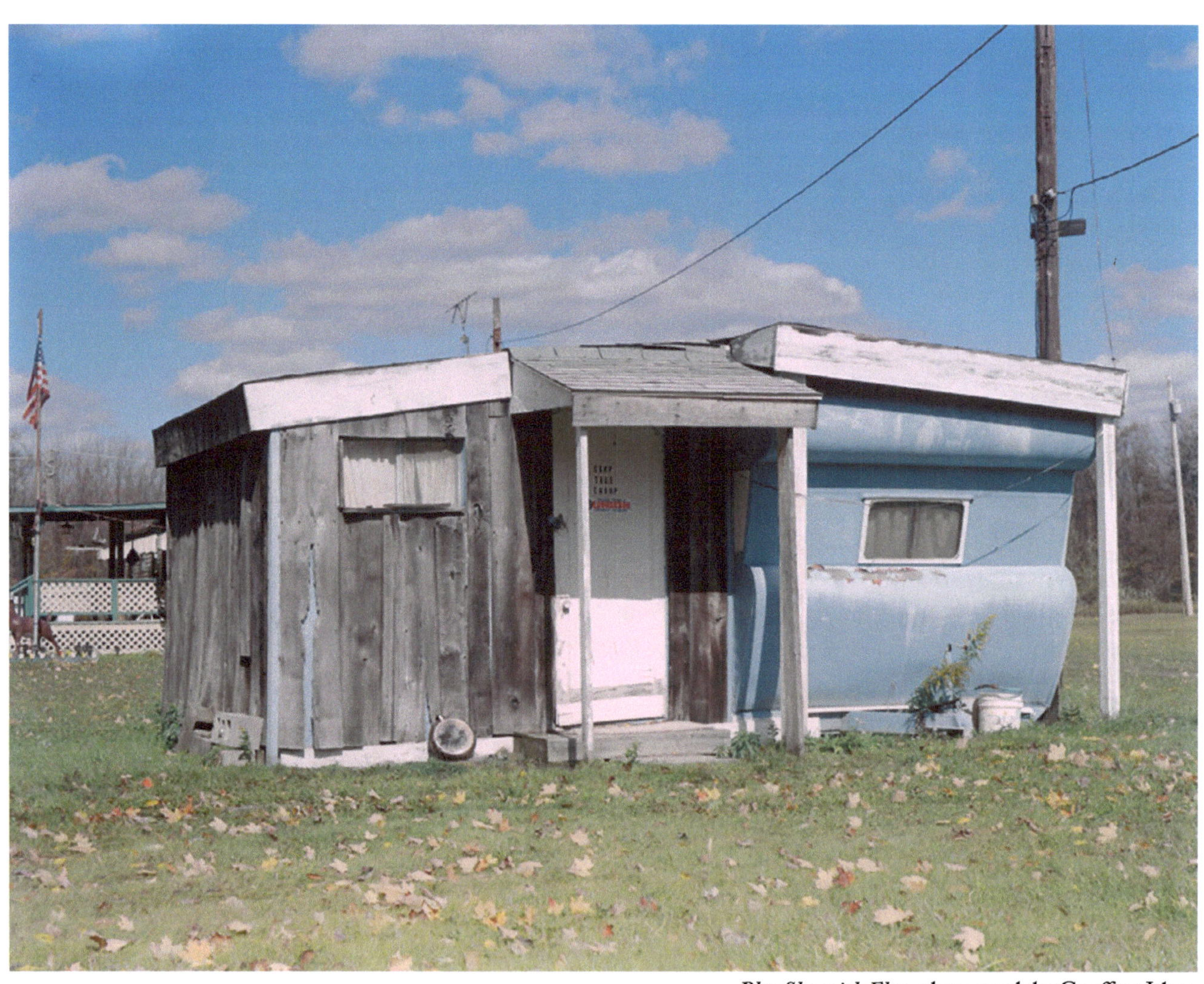

Blue Sky with Flag, **photograph by Geoffrey Ithen**

says, backhanding me in the chest. I laugh. For a second, I forget that I came back to sell my dad's house.

"Oh, jeez," Vin's mom says when she sees me come into her kitchen.

She looks ancient and acts surprised, like Vin's old friends always pop in and give her a hard time, but she was waiting with a casserole dish with some kind of lasagna in it, all warm and ready to eat almost an hour before midnight. I kiss her on the cheek and hug her around the neck because her huge old lady boobs get in the way and I want to be polite.

Vin taps me on the back of the head and stomps upstairs. I wonder if he has his own place or if he's been staying here at his mom's. I imagine that it's some sort of combination.

"Sit with me. You can stay a minute and talk, Jimmy. Be polite."

"Of course, Ms. V."

"You hungry?"

"Yeah, a little."

Vin's mom pushes me into a chair. Then she sways around the range trying to shovel out a neat square of lasagna that slides apart when it gets to the table. I tell her about my job and how I work in an office where I do sales stuff over the internet.

"Oh yeah?" she says, as if selling something over the internet is clever. "You ever do eBay? I do eBay. I sold a box of Vincent's grandmother's stuff, but they said I had to bring it all the way to the post office. What a hassle."

#

It's about one in the morning. Vin and I just drank our second pitcher of beer. I took a piss but I still feel really full so I go outside for a cigarette. The Narragansett beer sign in the bar window is really bright. It makes my reflection look goonier than it really is, but no one seems to notice. There aren't many people outside anyway, or there's more space, or I don't know.

Vin comes outside holding his cell phone to his ear. He has these puffy eyes now, which I've seen on older blue-collar guys when they drink or are tired. I don't like that look on his face. It makes him look spent, and I know the night will end before it really even begins and I'll have to go back to my dad's house.

"Who's that on the phone?" I ask. "Mike McCarran." Vin snaps his cell shut.

"No shit? How's he doing?"

"Real good. He married a girl from Saugus and he cuts lumber."

"Are they out doing something?"

"Nah, they're home with their little girl. Hey, gimme a cigarette."

I give him one of my Parliaments and light it for him. He breathes fast, trying to enjoy the first breath quickly.

"OK, I'll be right back. Going out to the car."

He gives the smoke back and shuffles down the block. I want to ask him about his sister again when he gets back because I want to see her. Not like before, I just want to see somebody I used to know. He and I have been wasting time at the bar just bullshitting about these people, but I really want to see them.

Although I'm not a particularly cheery guy, I want to watch their expressions brighten when they see me because I remind them of a time in their lives when they were younger. Even if I didn't even know them all that well and my face is just a kind of prop in their memory. Shit, it's been long enough. I feel like I've earned that.

Vin comes back from the car holding a plastic irregularly shaped case with a strap and we go back into the bar. He orders two shots of something you

The camera is an old heavy analogue and its black dials and levers look complicated. I fiddle with some of them but I have no idea what I'm doing or what the little white symbols mean.

plop into a pint glass. I say, "I'm really full," but he tells me to sack up and we both down them. I feel like I have a sea of mostly ineffective alcohol in my stomach. The lasagna floats upward, splitting apart slowly like a diagram of the earth.

"That was for your pop," Vin says. Then he slides the case over to me. I look at him and he's wondering why I don't already know what it is. I click open the top part of the hard shell which hinges back to reveal the components inside.

"Why are you giving me a camera, Vin?"

"You don't remember this one? Your dad gave me this one," he says, breathing heavily out of his nostrils. He says "this one" like there were a litter of cameras born from a bigger camera somewhere and we picked this one special. He puts an elbow on the bar and rests his head in his hand and looks at it, not touching it.

I can't recollect my dad ever being into photography. The man spent all his time pulling up lobster pots around Buzzards Bay. When he worked a desk at the harbormaster's sorting schedules he still never had any hobbies or anything apart from watching whatever game was on and taking mom out to dinner on Sunday.

"Vin, you sure?" I ask with a doubtful tone. But he thinks I'm asking if he's OK with giving it to me, not whether it was actually my dad's camera.

"Yeah, man. No problem. There are some rolls of film at the bottom of the case from when he gave it to me."

The camera is an old heavy analog and its black dials and levers look complicated. I fiddle with some of them but I have no idea what I'm doing or what the little white symbols mean. There is a second lens in a fuzzy compartment inside the case, separate from the one attached to the camera body. I have a hard time picturing my dad even using a camera, much less one that needed two lenses. The thought of him in a store deciding to buy an expensive piece of equipment, a piece that uses not one but two lenses, boggles my mind.

"My dad?" I ask aloud, almost as if Vin might be mistaken.

"Yeah, man. He gave it to me when I was visiting him in hospice. We looked at some of those National Geographic magazines together and he started talking about how convoluted some of them photo shoots are. Like, how those dudes get all the way out in some rainforest in the middle of Buttfuckia just to get one picture. Then, bam, he just up and gives me his camera. Maybe he thought I was you and wanted to be a photographer or something."

I feel like I don't know my dad anymore. How was I not there to receive something like this? How was I supposed to know this was coming my way? If I didn't know this about my dad, then what am I doing pretending and hanging out with fucking Vin here? I get mad and I can't understand why.

I must have had this look on my face like Vin stepped over some sort of line, because he says, "No, hey, look, man I was just holding onto it. I didn't use it or nothing. I didn't even take the caps off the lenses, 'cause I know the dust is bad for them."

Later, maybe like even a few years later, I'm cleaning out my apartment in L.A. and find this camera again, in the back of my closet where I left it.

I think about how my dad's house is long gone. Well, not gone, but sold to another family living there now. I wonder how they're using the driveway and if they tore up that fucking bush.

On the way to the office, I find a pharmacy that still develops film to get those film rolls at the bottom of the case developed. When I get them back, there are a few shots that are just white, as if someone was experimenting with shooting. I think at first that maybe Vin actually did try to use the camera. I hope to see some shots of the Lloyd Center with Vin karate-kicking through stuff. I don't see that, though.

At the bottom of the stack, there are some old, grainy pictures of the lawn in front of dad's house, shot from the street. The colors are all tinted blue and brown and the windows on the house have the old awnings on them. I see my mother gardening on the side of the house where the bush grew. Behind her, on one side of the driveway, I am jumping through a sprinkler.

Contributors

Larissa Shmailo's work has appeared or is forthcoming in *Gargoyle, Barrow Street, Drunken Boat, Fulcrum, Rattapallax, Jacket, The Unbearables Big Book of Sex*, and the Penguin anthology *Words for the Wedding*. Her books of poetry are *In Paran* (BlazeVOX [books]), the chapbook *A Cure for Suicide* (Cervena Barva Press, with foreword by Philip Nikolayev), and the e-book *Fib Sequence* (Argotist Ebooks). Larissa recently won honorable mention in the international Russian literary translator's competition for the Compass Award sponsored by Princeton University; her original translation of A. Kruchenych's "Victory over the Sun" is archived at the Museum of Modern Art (MoMA), the Los Angeles County Museum of Art, and the Smithsonian, and may be read at the *Brooklyn Rail's* InTranslation site: http://intranslation.brooklynrail.org/russian/victory-over-the-sun. She blogs at http://larissashmailo.blogspot.com/.

Susan Scutti grew up in Woodbridge, NJ and has lived in NYC since the late '80s. She writes poems, stories and novels. Most recently, Paper Kite Press published her full-length poetry collection, *The Commute,* and Ravenrock Press published her novel, *The Deceptive Smiles of Bredmeyer Deed* (with artwork by Sarah Valeri).

Samuel Ray Delany, Jr., also known as Chip, is an American author, professor and literary critic. His work includes a number of novels, many in the science fiction genre, as well as memoir, criticism, and essays on sexuality and society. He has published several autobiographical and semiautobiographical accounts of his life as a black, gay, and highly dyslexic writer, including his Hugo Award–winning autobiography, *The Motion of Light in Water.* In one of his nonfiction books, *Times Square Red, Times Square Blue* (1999), he draws on personal experience to examine the relationship between the effort to redevelop Times Square and the public sex lives of working-class men, gay and straight, in New York City. The later novels *The Mad Man, Hogg* and *Phallos* can be considered pornography, a label Delany himself endorses. *The Mad Man* and *Phallos* are linked with his 2012 novel, *Through the Valley of the Nest of Spiders*, his most recent book. His science fiction novels include *Babel-17, The Einstein Intersection, Nova, Dhalgren,* and the *Return to Nevèrÿon* series. After winning four Nebula Awards and two Hugo Awards over the course of his career, Delany was inducted into the Science Fiction Hall of Fame in 2002. Between 1988 and 1999, he was a professor of comparative literature at the University of Massachusetts Amherst. Between 1999 and 2000, he was a professor of English at SUNY Buffalo. Since January 2001 he has been a professor of English and creative writing at Temple University in Philadelphia, where he is director of the graduate creative writing program.

Anna Mockler's story collection *Burning Salt* (StringTown Press) was published in 2004. Her fiction has appeared in *Brooklyn Rail, Exquisite Corpse, Crab Creek Review, Raven Chronicles, Dial, Smoking Poet, Oxygen* and *Point No Point*. Other fiction was included in *The Unbearables Big Book of Sex* (2011, Unbearable Books/Autonomedia), *The Worst Book I Ever Read* (2009, *ibid.*), *Wreckage of Reason: Anthology of XXperimental Prose by Women Writers* (2008, Spuyten Duyvil) and *Dogs Cats Crows* (2001, Black Heron). She was born in New York and has lived all over the country, where she performed the traditional jobs of a writer: factory worker, office temp, waitress, printer, cabdriver, and restoration ecologist. She lives in Brooklyn.

Jesús Ángel García is a writer, musician and filmmaker based in San Francisco. "Sodomy Is a Threat to National Security: Fourth of July Weekend in Gethsemane" is adapted from his debut novel *badbadbad* (New Pulp Press). García is one-third of Three Times Bad, a dirty American roots-music string trio spunoff from the book's original soundtrack. The band plans to release its first album after the end of the world in the summer of 2013. The *badbadbad* documentary film—based on the novel's themes of fear, hypocrisy, intimacy in electronic culture, sexual morality and self-destruction—was an Official Selection of the 2012 Indie Fest USA International Film Festival. You can find all things 3xbad at: badbadbad.net and threetimesbad.com.

Amman Sabet is a designer and writer who vacillates between San Francisco and New York. He has published a smattering of poetry and cultivates a mattress novel in earnest, but won't quit his day job (whatever that is).

Throughout the '80s and '90s, **John Lurie** led the legendary band the Lounge Lizards. He recorded 22 albums and the soundtracks for over 20 films, including *Get Shorty*, which earned him a Grammy nomination. As an actor, he had starring roles in the Jim Jarmusch films, *Stranger than Paradise* and *Down by Law*, and supporting roles in Wim Wenders' *Paris, Texas*; Martin Scorsese's *The Last Temptation of Christ* and David Lynch's *Wild at Heart*, as well as a regular role on the HBO series *Oz*. Lurie wrote, directed and starred in the critically acclaimed television series, *Fishing with John*. For over thirty years, Lurie has been drawing and painting, yet only in the last eight years has he chosen to exhibit his work. In 2004, Lurie had his first painting exhibition at Anton Kern Gallery, New York. The Museum of Modern Art in New York and the Wadsworth Atheneum in Connecticut have acquired his work for their permanent collections. Lurie has published two collections of his work: *Learn to Draw*, a compilation of black and white drawings, and *A Fine Example of Art*, a full-color collection of over 80 reproductions.

Fred Frith is a songwriter, composer, improviser and multi-instrumentalist best known for the reinvention of the electric guitar that began with his solo album *Guitar Solos* in 1974. He learned his craft as both improviser and composer playing in rock bands, notably Henry Cow, and creating music in the recording studio. Much of his compositional output has been commissioned by choreographers and filmmakers, but his work has also been performed by Ensemble Modern, Hieronymus Firebrain, Arditti Quartet, Ground Zero, Robert Wyatt, Bang on a Can All Stars, Concerto Köln, and Rova Sax Quartet, among many others. He continues to perform internationally, most recently with Lotte Anker, Evelyn Glennie, Chris Cutler, John Zorn, Eye to Ear (a septet performing selections from his film music) and his latest band, Cosa Brava, whose most recent CD, *The Letter*, was released in 2012 to critical acclaim. Fred is the subject of Nicolas Humbert and Werner Penzels' award-winning documentary film, *Step Across the Border.* For the latest news and information about him, visit www.fredfrith.com

Doug Rice is the author of the forthcoming *Between Appear and Disappear* as well as *Dream Memoirs of a Fabulist, Blood of Mugwump, Skin Prayer* and *A Good Cuntboy Is Hard to Find.* His work has appeared in numerous anthologies and journals. He is currently an artist-in-residence at Akademie Schloss Solitude, in Stuttgart, and teaches at Sacramento State University.

Bradley Spinelli has herded cattle, worked on Wall Street and run away with the circus. His novel, *Pirate's Alley,* was a semifinalist in the Faulkner Competition. His play *Elusive* was presented by the National New Playwrights Network in Denver and received a staged reading at 13th Street Rep (NYC). His short fiction has been published by Sparkle Street and by Le Chat Noir ("Eyes of DeLillo," 2010), which also published an excerpt from the novel, *Killing Williamsburg,* in the collection *Drinking with Papa Legba* (2011). He lives with his wife in Brooklyn.

Marty Thau attended New York University from 1956 to 1960 and studied communication arts. After spending the latter half of the '60s as an award-winning record industry executive (Cameo-Parkway and Buddah Records), Thau forsook a cushy position with a mainstream production company (Van Morrison, John Cale, Miriam Makeba) to manage the rebirth of rock & roll in the form of the New York Dolls in the early '70s. Thau was integral to the development of New York's underground rock demimonde that evolved into a spawning ground of punk and new wave stars, and he is acknowledged as such in the *Encyclopedia of Record Producers,* a reference book that deals with the behind-the-scenes heroes of popular music. He worked with the Ramones, Blondie, Brian Setzer and Richard Hell, and produced Suicide, the Real Kids, the Fleshtones, and Martin Rev for his Red Star Label. These days, his time is spent licensing his music and writing his memoir. He was born and raised in NYC and now lives in Virginia near his daughter Leslie and two grandsons.

Jenny Wade is a musician (previous bands include Rude Buddha, Vodka, Swans, Timber) and has a Master's Degree in Russian Literature from Columbia University. She likes to translate the great Russian poets in the morning while having her tea. She lives with her husband and two daughters in California's Bay Area.

Chris Bava is an American photographer who lived and worked in Tijauana, Mexico. He was a former heroin trafficker who served 8 years in Federal prison following a worldwide sting operation in the late 1980s. Chris also struggled with addiction before and after his stint in prison, which eventually motivated him to move to Tijuana, to seek out alternative cures. You can learn more about Chris and his fascinating life and work by watching a feature-length documentary, produced as part of the Exile Nation Project, available at: http://vimeo.com/38354777.

J.D. King is a graphic artist, experimental musician and writer living in upstate NY. Recent illustration clients include *The New York Times, The Boston Globe,* the US Postal Service, *Audubon Magazine, The Washington Post, The Baffler,* and *P.I.M.* His band, J.D. King & The Coachmen, have two high-energy avant-rock albums out on Ecstatic Peace.

James Romberger is an American fine artist and cartoonist known for his depictions of New York City's Lower East Side. Romberger's pastel drawings of the ravaged landscape of the Lower East Side and its citizens are in many public and private collections, including the Metropolitan Museum of Art and Brooklyn Museum. For a long time, Romberger has been contributing work in the comics medium, including *Seven Miles A Second*, Romberger and Marguerite Van Cook's collaboration with artist, writer, and AIDS activist, David Wojnarowicz. Romberger is also a critic and writer for *Publisher's Weekly* and the comics blog the *Hooded Utilitarian.*

Ghazi Barakat is a German-Palestinian musician, journalist and subversive-art aficionado living in Berlin. He is currently making meta music for meta people in a meta world under the monicker of Pharoah Chromium and testing toxins from cold-blooded animal species for the "new drug revolution."

Sensitive Skin Books

on sale now at Amazon.com and select bookstores!

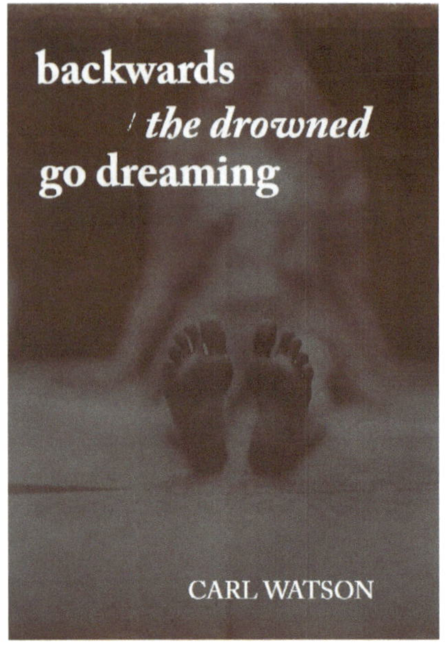

"[Watson] writes like someone who pushed himself to the wall, then pushed through it to the void and came back with stories to tell. Here he reclaims the Seventies, one of the more desolate of recent epochs, with the clarity of Proust, the balefulness of Bodenheim, and the raw honesty of an Iggy song."

—John Strausbaugh, author of *Black Like You* and *Sissy Nation*

"With prose unfurling like cigarette smoke bleeding into that cloud of half-forgotten memories forever shadowing missed opportunities that hangs over a noonday dive somewhere during the twilight of the last blown century, heartbreak rock-n-roll on the radio crackling in exquisite precision between am stations and windswept interstates, Carl Watson daydreams before silent black-and-white televisions in SRO lobbies or as he drinks himself sober in crumbling Chicago tenements. *Backwards the Drowned Go Dreaming* explodes the bleary-eyed myth of the American road."

—Donald Breckenridge, author of *This Young Girl Passing*

"Carl Watson's work is desolate poetry. He writes with sharp nostalgia for a past that really wasn't all that great. It feels like a stay in a down-and-out motel, but right on the other side of the paper-thin wall is transcendence. Watson never lets you forget that even in the most desperate situations, there is humor (even if it's mostly black) and greatness of the spirit."

—Emily XYZ, contributor, *United States of Poetry*

Black & White on Paper | 6" x 9" | 238 pgs. | ISBN/EAN13: 0983927146 / 978-0983927143 | List: $15.95

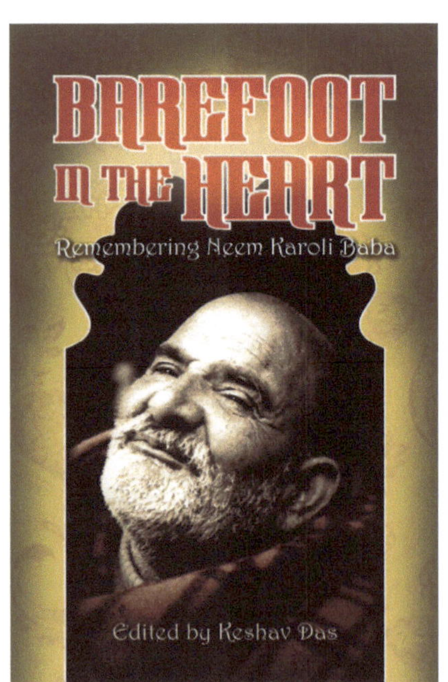

Barefoot in the Heart is a collection of transcribed oral stories of the Indian saint Neem Karoli Baba (Maharaji). It includes many anecdotes and first-person retellings of stories collected in India and in the USA over a period of 9 years by Keshav Das, including a small selection of unpublished stories originally intended for inclusion in *Miracle Of Love* by Ram Dass.

"*Barefoot In The Heart* is a divine raft to take us across the ocean of darkness to the glorious land of light. Every page is filled with Maharaji's nectar. Profound gratitude to Keshav Das and his collaborators."

—Jai Uttal

Black & White on Paper | 6" x 9" | 168 pgs. | ISBN-13/ISBN-10: 978-0983927129/ 098392712X | List: $15.95

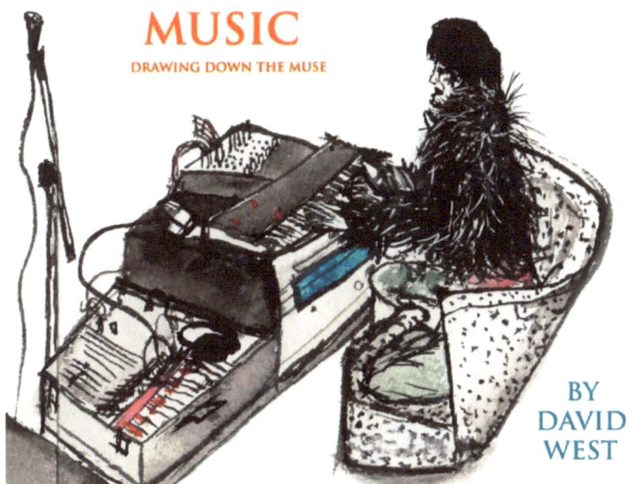

"Inside this book you get *portraiture vérité* of bands in action. Banging away in rehearsal. The appreciative eye watching the battle of the bands as they try to navigate their way through the sometimes complicated maze of illusions, delusions and solutions of grandeur before asphyxiation and evaporation of all the notes into the air. I'm the wrong person to comment on rehearsal as I work in a more backward way. I don't care if a performance is anally-retentive-perfect because a computer can do that now. I'll work hard on something to a point then I stop, as what I want surprises myself, especially in a live situation. It's a viewpoint probably not shared by most of the bands in this book but that's what makes things interesting. It's up to others to state theirs and that takes us to the artist.

"David West hits the target dead center BOOM with his beautifully liquid renderings of NYC bands in rehearsal. Mr. West captures a scene in the late 1990s largely ignored. These aren't vacuous American Idols but musicians who are The Real Deal. Like a fly on the wall, David gives you an inside view from his own multifaceted eye. There is a dripping aquatic fluidity to his drawings. Mr. West is not afraid to let the ink, gouache, and watercolor run and flow, never betraying the nature of his medium. That's why he's The Real Deal. If you the viewer can't understand, appreciate and see that in his work then go out and get corrective eye surgery!"

—Monte Cazazza of Psychic TV

Full Color Bleed on White paper | 8" x 7" | 110 pgs. | ISBN/EAN13: 0983927170 / 978-0983927174 | List: $24.95

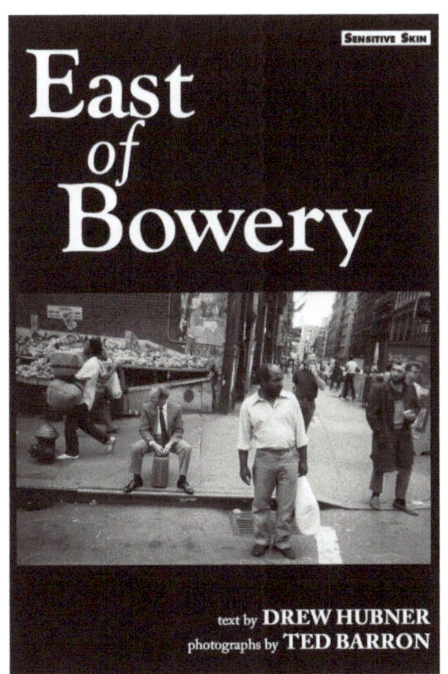

East of Bowery began as a collaborative web project between writer Drew Hubner (*American by Blood, We Pierce*) and photographer Ted Barron in 2008. It was subsequently performed as a multimedia performance with live musical accompaniment at The Gershwin Hotel and The Bowery Poetry Club. This is the first print publication of the project.

"Drew Hubner's prose and Ted Barron's photos are kin, at once raw and lyrical, grit and grace, which is what the city was like back then. The combination is magic, the essence of the time and place."

—Luc Sante, author of *Low Life* and *Kill All Your Darlings*

"*East of Bowery* is a sharply focused, street-level view of Downtown before the real estate agents started renaming everything."

—Steve Earle, author of *Doghouse Roses* and *I'll Never Get out of This World Alive*

"Drew Hubner writes like people used to."

—William Georgiades, *New York Magazine*

"The voice is loose, jazzy, and fast, the memories liquid and hot, avoiding the romance of macho drug memoirs with black humor, verisimilitude and a knack for the absurd."

—Kate Christensen, author of *In the Drink* and *The Astral*

Black & White on Paper | 6" x 9" | 154 pgs. | ISBN/EAN13: 0983927103 / 9780983927105| List: $15.95

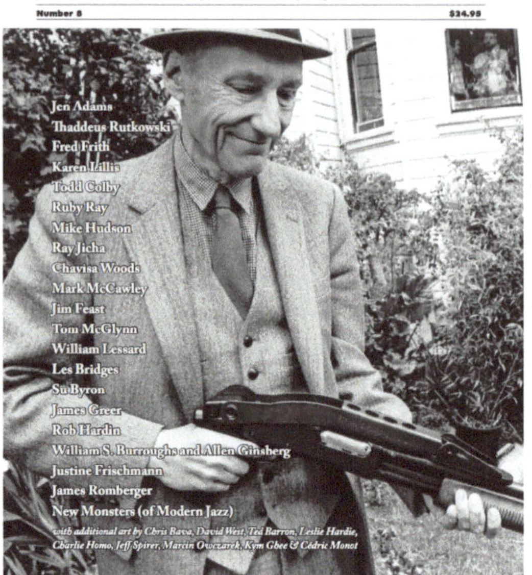

SENSITIVE SKIN #8

on sale at Amazon.com and select bookstores

Featuring a rarely seen interview with **William S. Burroughs** by **Allen Ginsberg**.

With iconic punk photographs by **Ruby Ray**, art by **Tom McGlynn** and **Justine Frischmann**, music by **The New Monsters**, a comic written and drawn by **James Romberger**, writing by **Mike Hudson, James Greer, Thaddeus Rutkowski, Chavisa Woods, Jim Feast, Mark McCawley, Todd Colby**, and much more.

Full Color on White Paper | 8.5" x 11" | 118 pgs. | ISBN-13: 978-0983927150 | ISBN-10: 0983927154 | List: $24.95

Other things you might enjoy, if this is the kind of thing you like.

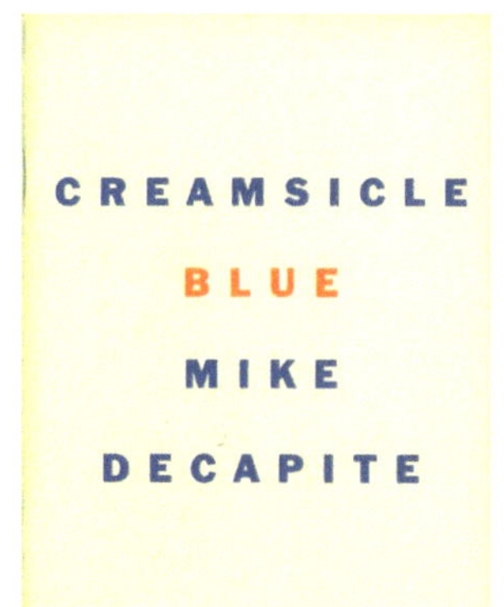

"*Creamsicle Blue* is a spectacular piece of writing."

—Karen Lillis, author of *Watch the Doors as They Close*

"I'm excited about this form. *Creamsicle Blue* is as close as I've gotten to the kind of thing I've always wanted to do."

—Mike DeCapite

$10 postage-paid at www.sparklestreet.com

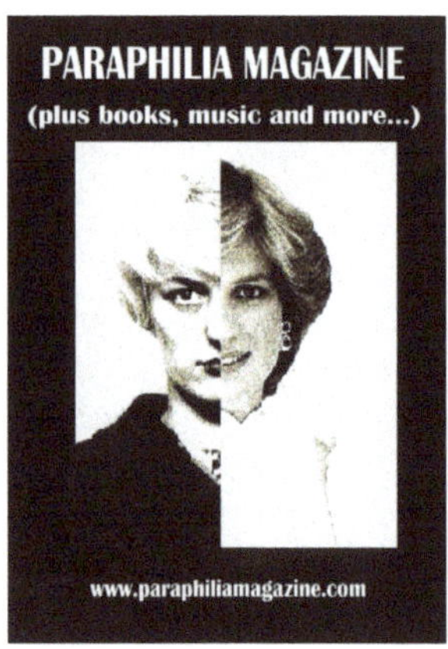

Paraphilia is an unlicensed, underground enterprise that renounces established and arbitrary rules, regulations, guidelines, genres, categories, and all other manmade shackles. *Paraphilia* recognizes that expression is a fundamental function of the human organism and, within these walls, it will only be presented in the purest, rawest, most unfettered form. The sole requirement for admission is an open mind, so do come in, we embrace your presence.